The Interpretation
of Owls

The Interpretation of Owls

Selected Poems, 1977–2022

John Greening
edited by Kevin J. Gardner

BAYLOR UNIVERSITY PRESS

Cover image and frontispiece: Untitled, by Clarence Melville Greening (1901)
Cover and book design by Kasey McBeath

Library of Congress Cataloging-in-Publication Data

Names: Greening, John, 1954- author. | Gardner, Kevin J., editor.
Title: The interpretation of owls : selected poems, 1977-2022 / John
    Greening ; edited by Kevin Gardner.
Other titles: Interpretation of owls (Compilation)
Description: Waco, Texas : Baylor University Press, [2023] | Summary: "A substantial
    selection from the work of distinguished British poet John Greening, featuring
    poems from forty-five years arranged thematically, and including author interview,
    introductory material, and indexes."-- Provided by publisher.
Identifiers: LCCN 2022050484 | ISBN 9781481317344 (hardback)
Subjects: LCGFT: Poetry.
Classification: LCC PR6057.R373 I58 2023 | DDC 821/.914--dc23/eng/20221121
LC record available at https://lccn.loc.gov/2022050484

Contents

Reaching the Stillness

An Introduction by the Editor

It was while sifting through contemporary poetry journals a few years ago that I first encountered the work of John Greening. I was editing an anthology of elegies about English parish churches when I discovered his poem about the church in Little Gidding famed for its association with George Herbert and Nicholas Ferrar. I was immediately struck by the unique stance he took in response to the querulous laments Larkin poses in "Church Going" about the future of churches: what shall we "turn them into"? shall we "avoid them as unlucky places," perhaps keep a few "chronically on show"? Greening's poem (you may read it in its entirety on p. 38) offers a witty diversion from the usual elegiac brooding about a declining faith and instead addresses a pressing, new concern:

> When the man in the four-by-four attempted to winch off
> the lightning conductor from Little Staughton spire for the copper,
> was that the beginning of the final act? Iconoclasts move
> beyond stained glass and altar screens: they strike
> at Michelangelo's very finger and bring down the roof.

Despite the geographical specificity, this is no insular Little Englandism; Greening's perspective is not to savor the obscurity and remoteness of rural England in isolation from the world. Instead he renders such places familiar by establishing kinship with European and global culture. He abjures English reclusiveness as much as he abhors heritage crime, implying that a criminal disregard of culture and history adheres to those with isolationist tendencies, while those who look to the world develop a keen sensitivity to history and beauty and their preservation. Instead of pondering the significance of an empty church, Greening asks us to consider the wanton vandalism of a work of art. To steal materials from a church roof not only reenacts the iconoclasm of the churchmanship of

Edward VI or Oliver Cromwell; it also severs the tender touch of divine and human fingers and breaks that connective spark of creation.

Greening's poem about Little Gidding typifies in many ways his understanding of temporal experience. Time is a series of geological layers, with the here and now a thin veneer atop the past's strata of varying colors, thicknesses, and substances. It isn't Larkin that will help us appreciate Greening, but Eliot. I think of Eliot's metaphor, in his own *Little Gidding*: "The moment of the rose and the moment of the yew-tree / Are of equal duration." History is a layering of eternal moments, and when the poet peels back each mantle, we experience each moment at once; the past, whether "real" or imagined, is always present. When I queried John about this resonance between his vision and Eliot's, he readily admitted, "he's at the source of everything for me." At the source: it's absolutely essential to understand that all poets have a Helicon at the base of which the sacred springs bubble forth; from thence the poet journeys forward.

In reading poetry, we often experience a temporal or spatial dislocation. In one of his earliest poems, "Westerners" (which gave the title to his first collection of poetry back in 1982), John dislocates us in a journey that carries us from England to Egypt, from modern comforts to ancient treasure, from immediate present to remote past, and from living to dead. The poem (which can be read in full on p. 51) reverses the Eurocentric pattern of the goggle-eyed traveller staring in bemusement at the cultural other. He expresses a sense of wonder in travelling to Upper Egypt in the late 1970s, and reimagines the sheer excitement at being one of the few Europeans there at the time, but realizes that it is surely he who is strange. The poem establishes a kind of doubling effect that is a common feature of his verse. The "westerners," of course, are the expatriate poet and his wife, but for the Ancient Egyptians "westerners" were the dead, since they buried them on the West Bank of the Nile. Such layering and duality defines his work and lends it much of its subtle richness. Eliot again: "So I assumed a double part, and cried / And heard another's voice cry, 'What! are *you* here?'"

As in "Westerners," much of Greening's poetry adumbrates a global perspective that takes his readers well beyond the boundaries of Great Britain, a noteworthy characteristic that sets his work apart from that of other modern British poets. Perhaps because he has travelled so widely and has lived throughout the world, his poetic perspective is, quite literally, a worldview. When I immersed myself in his work with an eye toward a thematically arranged selection, there was an almost natural gravitation toward sorting poems by their setting—Egypt, England, America and so forth. I confessed to John that I was chary of labelling him a poet of place. "But I am a poet of place," he rightly admonished me. More accurate to say, though, that he is a poet of places, a singer of significant soil. To read this collection in its entirety from start to finish is in essence to be taken on a fabulous journey. Almost the entire book is about inhabiting other places or coming home to an unexpected otherness after being in other places; it's about being transported to other worlds, by poetic, musical, and numinous encounters.

In the opening section we see the poet as "Pilgrim" and accompany him through an array of spiritual experiences, from institutional religion to something less defined or attached. Yet there is always a willing ear attuned to the divine, an attentiveness that Eliot describes in *The Dry Salvages* as "The silent listening to the undeniable / Clamour of the bell of the last annunciation." In the second section, John's pilgrimage metamorphoses into something more literal as we follow him to Egypt, where he goes as a volunteer and teacher in Aswan. Here in "Hieroglyphs," he is not only a traveller in an antique land but an archaeologist *manqué*, opening tombs and awakening the ancient dead to tell their stories. And when the poet and his wife return to England, they bring Egypt with them, having been altered forever by their encounters. "Home" then explores not England as such, but a sense of what *home* means; here we see scenes of the poet's suburban life as a son, husband, father, and teacher, as well as of his boyhood life on Hounslow Heath, outside London.

How apt are Eliot's lines in *East Coker*: "Home is where one starts from. As we grow older / The world becomes stranger, the pattern more complicated / Of dead and living." Having lived in Egypt, the poet sees England in an entirely new way, and this fourth section, "English," explores England's history, its landscape, and its people in startling portrayals of temporal dislocation. The urge to escape leads to "Flight," a frequent theme and subject in his work—understandable for one who grew up under the Heathrow flight path. Such flights carry the poet and reader thence to "America," comprising meditations on his sojourn on this continent and through its violent history. Considering the rather militaristic histories of our country and his own, it will not surprise us that life in "Wartime" is a recurring subject of John's poetry. In this section, not only do we encounter grim reminders of war just below the glossy overlay of civilization; we sense that to live in the here and now is to live with both the memory and the ever-present reality of war.

Thoughts of Europe scarred by combat lead us to contemplate Greening's "Eurozone," an imaginative landscape across the permeable borders of the continent through settings and scenes that range from an Irish jail to a Roman fountain to a Salzburg concert hall, from the tectonic plates of Iceland to the beaches of Crete, all crowned with a remarkable crown of sonnets—fifteen interlocking sonnets contemplating (pre-Brexit) the idea of a European Union. That sequence reminds us of Greening's range and versatility as a poet and his exceptional dexterity of form—not only sonnets but villanelles, sestinas, shaped poems, long lines, short lines, free verse, blank verse, syllabic verse, and an astounding facility with slant rhyme. "Only by the form, the pattern, / Can words or music reach / The stillness," writes Eliot in *Burnt Norton*. Unsurprising, then, that we are taken on flights through "Words" and "Notes," for there are few things in human experience that this poet loves more than poetry and music—those forces that transport us from the mundanity of the present and out of the dark layers of history into something resembling eternity. Other places, other worlds, and otherness: and so the journey ends with "Intimations" of eternity and the numinous. Something altogether other, and yet strangely like where the journey began. Eliot, again from *Little Gidding*:

> We shall not cease from exploration
> And the end of all our exploring
> Will be to arrive where we started
> And know the place for the first time.

Just as I was hesitant to label Greening a poet of place, so have I resisted labelling him a religious poet. "I would say I'm more religious than most contemporary British poets," John has countered. No doubt this is so. A British stereotype is reserve or reticence, and this is perhaps never more apposite than where religion is concerned; indeed religion is a music to which many poets have grown deaf. But Greening does think religiously, and he also writes religiously, though with indirection and without ever resembling a contemporary Herbert or Hopkins. One is not likely to uncover in his poetry an encounter on the Road to Damascus or find him wrestling with angels. Nevertheless, he looks at the world through a spiritual lens, treating creation as sacred and writing as one who perceives in life the mysterious workings of the divine. "Addressing the unknown—that's always been the business of poetry," he acknowledges in "Homecoming—To My Family" (read the whole poem, a translation of Hölderlin, on p. 169). The poet's greatest quest is to seek union with the eternal and the numinous, as he writes in "Walking" (p. 30), a poem of astonishing beauty and extraordinary simplicity:

> It is a rhythm that we require,
> that speaks of essences and immortality; not a pilgrimage
>
> because there is no aim, the route is circular, but a stay
> against age, climbing edge after edge.

Kevin Gardner
Waco, Texas

Two Roads

A Preface by the Author

A "Selected Poems" is always revealing, especially when the selecting is not done by the poet, and when it is for a readership unfamiliar with the work. It was only as Kevin Gardner began the editing process that I realised just how important American poetry has been to me. When I was about fourteen, we were asked by an English teacher to choose a poem we liked, and for some reason I opted for one by Howard Nemerov, "Brainstorm" from the *Faber Book of Modern Verse* (did someone give me that or did I buy it for myself?). I still have the mini essay I produced, which has at least the virtue of candour: "'Brainstorm'," I explain in the first paragraph, "gets rather complicated at points but I will give you my idea of what it means . . . ."

As a teenager, largely ignorant of poetry but instinctively drawn to it, I remember taking Wallace Stevens's *Collected* off the shelves at Hounslow Public Library. I must have liked the lofty-sounding mysteries of the work, much as Milton's 'grand style' would seduce me a few years later in the school Sixth Form. It was Robert Lowell who had a more enduring influence, notably his *For the Union Dead*, and I steadily bought all the volumes—yes, all the versions of *Notebook*. Frost I came to later, curiously enough, via his best friend, the English war poet, Edward Thomas. But I stumbled on a random selection of other Americans, sometimes because of an English connection, as with Denise Levertov (born in Essex) or Donald Hall (posted here during WW2), or later because I was asked to review them (Hayden Carruth), or heard them read (C. K. Williams) or responded to someone's recommendation (like Ted Hughes's of Anthony Hecht). James Merrill I first found in beautiful hardback Phoenix Living Poets editions remaindered in a Somerset bookshop, though it wasn't until 1990 when my family and I came to live in New Jersey that I read him properly.

It was during that Fulbright exchange year the flood-gates opened, and it was Helen Vendler's *Harvard Book of Contemporary American Poetry* helped direct the flow. I read Merrill's extraordinary *The Changing Light at Sandover*, came to love the work of Louise Glück and especially A. R. Ammons, both the "very short poems" and the crazy epics like *Tape for the Turn of the Year*, composed on a reel of adding-machine paper. A grateful student at the high school where I was teaching gave me Amy Clampitt's recently published *The Kingfisher* (what an enlightened choice). The very first book I bought when we arrived in Clinton, N.J.—it was one of the few poetry volumes in our tiny local bookshop—was in fact Howard Nemerov's *Collected*, and one day I even got the chance to hear him read at the Geraldine R. Dodge festival in Waterloo. He included his marvellous late Larkin elegy (this was shortly before his own death) and I briefly spoke with him, mentioning what an effect "Brainstorm" had had on me. Only now does it occur to me that "He sat alone / In an upstairs room and heard these things" must have had an especial potency for one growing up under the main flight path to Heathrow Airport. Anyway, Howard Nemerov said he thought it was a pretty dark way for a young man to be introduced to poetry.

There were other pilgrimages—to William Carlos Williams's Paterson, for instance, commemorated here in a poem I have never published before; and to T. S. Eliot's Gloucester, where I scanned the horizon for those Dry Salvages, prompting an uncollected poem we have included. Both Williams and Eliot have been hugely formative influences: in my twenties I learned *The Waste Land* off by heart to impress my future wife, but *Four Quartets* has long been the spiritual centre of my work, its lines carrying an authority and a power I dream of emulating. The only way I have managed to come close to "Little Gidding" is by actually living a stone's throw from the village, which features in several poems here. It is perhaps, as I shyly suggested to Seamus Heaney when I found myself talking with him beside Nicholas Ferrar's church in Gidding, my "omphalos." Before Jane and I settled in Huntingdonshire, when we were newly-wed teaching volunteers in Upper Egypt, it was William Carlos Williams who gave me a way of escaping Eliot's influence and capturing those intensely exotic scenes. You may notice some of his inflexions in the poems included here from my first collection, *Westerners*.

There have been subsequent visits to the USA, especially to Seattle where my sister-in-law lives, and where I insisted on dragging the family to Bainbridge Island, partly to see Chief Seattle's grave, but also because it's where Roethke died (his short-lived replacement in Seattle, Vernon Watkins, is a poet I value greatly too, not least because he is from Swansea). When my play about the Lindbergh kidnap was being performed in 2002 in Asheville, North Carolina, I was fascinated to spend time in an area so important to A. R. Ammons and more famously associated with the Black Mountain Poets. Robert Creeley I had discovered in my teens and his minimalism probably affects those early Egyptian poems as much as Williams's.

I have made many friends among American poets. How did I first meet Dana Gioia? I think he invited me to an event on the Hudson before he moved away, but I was unable to attend. Certainly I recall sitting in a library and lighting upon his controversial article "Can Poetry Matter?" in the May 1991 issue of *Atlantic Monthly*. Perhaps I wrote to him about it? Subsequently I came to know that great Alaskan sage, John Haines, the poet-mathematician Emily Grosholz, and the polymath Alfred Corn—Alfred was with me on a Hawthornden writers' retreat in 2010, and I was reminded of Browning: "Ah, did you once see Shelley plain?" This was someone who knew Lowell and had been a close friend of Merrill. I like to think that J. M. would have appreciated the masque I wrote for Alfred and the other Hawthornden residents to perform. Sylvia Plath's biographer, the poet Anne Stevenson, too became a very good friend, and she was living near us in Cambridge for a while. The shade of Sylvia Plath has never been far away during my writing life, from my early correspondence with Ted Hughes to my recent stint as a Writing Fellow at Plath's old college, Newnham, in Cambridge when I used to park my car next to her lodgings.

I would eventually write an entire book about American poetry since 1963, how it seems to be caught between the Wilderness and the Ouija board. It was never published but split into separate chapters among other books. This new selection of my own work is, perhaps, a way of acknowledging that debt at last. The real debt, however, is to my friend Kevin Gardner for devoting so much time and energy in preparing *The Interpretation of Owls*. It was during my visit to Baylor in 2018 to lecture on Edmund Blunden that we began collaborating on *Hollow Palaces*, our country house anthology. The idea of this *Selected* came rather later, and developed in parallel. Much of the discussion took place via email and WhatsApp during the coronavirus pandemic. I provided Kevin with a list of poems which were important to me, along with texts of suitable unpublished or uncollected poems, but he did the rest, and the final decisions have always been his. There has nevertheless been continual exchange of ideas about the selection since 2020. My last *Selected* was a very different book. Indeed, three quarters of the poems in *The Interpretation of Owls* were not included in *Hunts: Poems 1979–2009*, and well over a hundred have never been collected before. There is a whole clutch of previously unpublished verses written in America, and some of the more spiritually inclined work which I have been reticent to publish in the UK (where we are perhaps more sceptical and cynical) here finds a place. Kevin has also picked up on certain themes and preoccupations of mine—Egypt, of course, and Iceland, but Englishness too, war, flight, music, language itself. It is a great delight to me to see this book in print, and if nothing else I hope it may remind readers that although English and American poetry may sometimes feel like two diverging roads, we're all in the same wood.

John Greening
Stonely, Cambridgeshire

Acknowledgments

Thanks are due to the following individuals: David Aycock, Les Bell, Alan Brekin, Victoria Fox, Wolfgang Görtschacher, Harry Hasbrouck, Jenny Hunt, Cade Jarrell, Jim Kates, Kasey McBeath, Michelle McCaig, Cecilia McDowall, Dave Nelson, Michael Schmidt, Sheila Wakefield, and Elisabeth Wiedemann.

"Autumn Manoeuvres" is a translation from the German of "Herbstmanöver" by Ingeborg Bachmann and is translated and printed by kind permission of Dr. Heinz Bachmann and Piper Verlag. Ingeborg Bachmann, *Herbstmanöver* from: *Werke, Band 1* (© Piper Verlag GmbH, München/Berlin 1978).

"Mayflower: Three Expeditions" is extracted from *The Mayflower*, a sequence commissioned by Cecilia McDowall to be set to music, and is reproduced with the composer's kind permission. Ms. McDowall retains the rights to future musical settings of this work.

"Nicholas Ferrar and the Pilgrim" and "Castanea Sativa" appear as untitled sections of John Greening's pamphlet *The Giddings* (Mica Press, 2021) and are reprinted by kind permission of Leslie Bell (for Mica Press) and John Greening.

"From the Word-house," "Rhine Journey," and "Somersby" appear in *a Post Card to* (Red Squirrel Press, 2021) and are reprinted by kind permission of Sheila Wakefield and Red Squirrel Press.

"After the Interval," "Alive Alive O," "Strauss," and "Sibelius in Italy" (reprinted here as the second section of "Sibelius at Ainola") appear in *Moments Musicaux* (Poetry Salzburg, 2020) and are reprinted by kind permission of Wolfgang Görtschacher and Poetry Salzburg.

The following poems appear in *To the War Poets* (Carcanet, 2013) and are reproduced by kind permission of Carcanet Press, Manchester, UK:

"American Music"
"Awre"

"Causeway"
"Colonial"
"Eglwys Llangwyfan"
"Feast Day, Melchbourne"
"Field"
"Heath Row"
"Hounslow"
"In Trafalgar Square"
"New World (1937)"
"Odyssey"
"To August Stramm, Georg Trakl, Ernst Stadler, Georg Heym"
"To John McCrae"
"To Rupert Brooke"
"To the Sun"
"Yeats Dances: Part IV"

The following poems appear in *The Silence* (Carcanet, 2019) and are reproduced by kind permission of Carcanet Press, Manchester, UK:

"Airmail for Chief Seattle"
"Compleat"
"Flight Path"
"Fontevraud"
"Homecoming—To My Family"
"Hyperion's Song of Destiny"
from *The Silence*: the 16-line section beginning "A white-suited spectre"
   (reprinted here as the third section of "Sibelius at Ainola")

Permission to reprint copyrighted material as epigraphs to poems is as follows:

Excerpt from "Fall 1961" from *Collected Poems* by Robert Lowell. Copyright © 2003 by Harriet Lowell and Sheridan Lowell. Reprinted by permission of Farrar, Straus and Giroux.

Excerpt from "The Osprey" from *Collected Poems for Children* by Ted Hughes, pictures by Raymond Briggs. Text copyright © 2005 by The Estate of Ted Hughes. Reprinted by permission of Farrar, Straus and Giroux and by Faber and Faber Ltd.

The Interpretation
of Owls

Prelude

Huntingdonshire Psalmody

Along the last track my father rode his bike,
the last track my mother walked before the farmer
drove up and ordered us off the land, a lark

is singing what it's always sung, ethereal minstrel,
blithe spirit, not quite yet extinct.

.

A stand of elm, its branchlets rich in tiny flowers,
bisexual, reddish brown, all ready for their voyage.

They reach so far, some thirty feet, before
disease sets in. Is this the Wych Elm, the English,
or a Huntingdon variety? A red kite lurches,
delighting in its own resurgence, and the elms enthuse,

bejewelled, pretending they are all grown up, as old
as the ocean in this soft Sunday wind. There they go.

.

and there a solitary lark in the middle of the bare field

a brilliant silver piccolo natural trumpet fanfare

all baroque trills and decoration, broadcasting

across the pastoral world, higher still and higher

.

Quickthorn hurries me on to check if a favourite elm
that looked from a distance as though it had been buzzed
out of existence, has—it has, thank God—been pollarded only.

I learn to walk more slowly, to look
at the first mayflower,
below the birthplace
of the 'first American President'.

We live among such stories, mostly forgetting them.

I hope for hares, and have seen them
in the shadow of the Hoo,
its mythical Templar moat,
running, though never boxing.

This oak alone remembers what was here

before it was left to those crooked knees
and recurrently green tips,
shipwrecked in a field with its dreams
of sail, peeping at Grafham Water

and reaching for the easyJetting skies.

.

The signs with handmade arrows at the entrance to the farm
say CYCLES, although the indicated path will soon
run out into a rutted field no bike could master.

.

The smooth, the battered, the flinty sharp, a dog-biscuit piece of Anglo-Saxon, a medieval tile, some broken Roman Samian ware. Everything crumbles for the moment, although in a day it could all revert to fenny swamp, as these larks know—two of them now trying to outdo each other, following the record of the landscape, picking out their demisemiquavers from the remains of plainsong.

.

After so many shades of brown, the joy of a
cowslip lane, its tiny exhortations.

Behind it, a few bluebells
turn their faces down

as if to avoid some bruter
yellow they once had to endure.

.

The Nine Mad Maidens, as you call them, on the horizon,
could also be desperate swimmers escaping
a wrecked cargo of battery chickens
who have spotted that church they think is a lighthouse.

Where are they heading in a race that can never be won,
a mill race, in ever-decreasing circles,
a millionaires' race, with
ever-increasing sustaina-
and profita-
bility?

Or the one against time,
with ever-decreasing energy?

The wood they swim through is nameless,
and as calm as it can be under the circumstances.

.

Dead tyred, archaic agricultural equipment,
faded blue, rust streaked, under nettles.

Someone's beanie on a solitary fencepost.

An oil drum, the colour of fatigues, wrapped
in bramble, impossible to tell what it contained.

Pieces of gate that go back to Edward Thomas.

Perfectly round patches of ash on the field-edge
that overlooks the Pollards' house, and St Peter's church.

A slack electric cable trying to slither among the elms.

.

Always the larksong   morse   short-wave   messages
tuning   Save Our invisible Souls   an older way
as a helicopter   crosses itself   and the cracks open
in a line laid down by weedkiller among the nests

.

Praise be, someone is troubling to set
     a proper layered hedge on the ridge
         between Huntingdonshire and Bedfordshire—

a yellow Loadall is parked beside
     heaps of logs, and half-
         cut hawthorn and blackthorn are lovingly

laid from post to post ready to sprout.
     The lost language of pleaching.
         Someone has something to say for the land.

.

Beyond all this, of course, is

the solar farm, its tarot pack
laid out with a hundred

shifty winks. It tells us
the country's future, clean

elegy that knows the dark
web of profit and power

vested in so much praise.

You never see the exact location of a lark's nest

any more than you can pin them to a point
in the sky. First here, then gone. Sing on,

you larks, and keep turning through the turning
of the seasons, the soil, a distant ringing of the changes,

though your final plummet be inevitably silent.

The 'first American President' refers to Edward Maria Wingfield, who lived in Greening's Cambridgeshire village of Stonely. Wingfield was a founding member of the Virginia Company of London and the first president of the Council of Virginia. KG

Pilgrim

Changes

The bell-ringers resume their Monday evening practice,
their clashes and discords still a far cry from those engines

I used to hear being tested on the other side of my dreams,
the howling of an angry heathen god, when I was young.

Our daughter is halfway across the Arabian Sea from India,
the thunder of her crisis-ridden holiday not yet dispelled.

Between flights, in Dubai, she will hear perhaps the call
to prayer, that miraculous high trail, *allahu akbar.*

The time zones shift, clocks go forward and back.
A minaret from the seventh century, a spire from the fourteenth,

and the latest in-flight entertainment making its approach
through mist across the heath. *Spoilt!* cries the Captain

of the Bells, as a young girl tries to master the changes
and summon whatever soul is listening back to the aisles.

Bell

Imagine this bell in its mould
at Whitechapel, calling

across the centuries, its white
music molten still

but cooling, slowly, to an alloy—
copper and tin tuned

out of time's sand and hay
and horse manure: a pure

note rung like goodness from
the dung of history, from

a hemisphere whose call to prayer
was kept true by a crook.

Falling in Lent

It took a minister of the church
to cut our two cypresses down.
Invisible except for his power line
he droned from our neighbour's ladder

and once reached out for a branch
that did not exist and fell
unbelievably through my gaze on to
his back, clutching a bow saw

as if he were about to perform
Bach or the Devil's Trill and not
break his spine. He was fine,
thanks to faith—and leylandii fronds.

But I think of that fifteen-foot drop
into a winded silence as my daughters
sit whittling sailing boats out of
clippings from his legendary fall.

'I wanted to tell you I was all right
but I didn't have the breath,' he laughed
and launched back up the ladder
where now there is only air

and pigeons fluttering their responses
to the pulpit stump preaching
steadfastness, incensed by the hunger
of a fire that has lasted forty days.

They

They went into a dream that only occasionally calls here
They went into a mountainscape of paths and fertile terraces
They had climbed aboard a moving train towards the interior
They departed without luggage and left you on the platform

With a cold water bottle and a blanket to be tucked in
With acetate, oxide and celluloid in your suitcase
With a number that gave sad answers, a distant crossing
With certain habits, odd beliefs, and a way of saying

You carry with you as you make your own preparations
You hold for inspection as a tunnel darkens the window
You keep, so when your cortege draws up at a jetty
You are not just another dry-leaf cousin in the bardo

But their own son they planted and raised and watched over
But trained to bear on hard paths and hostile terraces
But never hurt, encouraging, enriching, set loose
But harvest now, who's ready for them to consume his shining

Elegy

Perhaps it will be like this: a mist hanging across
a landscape almost familiar, and an empty lane,
on each side a signpost indicating a footpath—

the one down to where the old Priory once stood,
to the remains of a fresh well and some hallowed
stones, to the half-moon of an Augustinian moat

lost in the clay and sprouting shoots of winter wheat,
no track, but a field where there has been a bull,
no sound but the drop of water into the depths.

The other path leads up across a stile and into the long
grass, through and past the sheep and over into
a huge open space where, on a mistless day,

the reservoir will catch the eye a mile or two away.

Hyperion's Song of Destiny

Hölderlin: 'Hyperions Schicksalslied'

You tread the light fantastic
   on your sprung boards, holy dancers of the soul.
      Heavenly weather teases
         you, its breezes
           like fingertips of a harpist
            drawing sacred scales.

Unmoved by fate as a sleeping
   newborn, the immortal ones breathe
      safely snug
         in their budding, suitably
         aired, their spirits
           eternally
            in flower and their holy eyes
              looking with peaceful
              clarity for good.

But we have no such luck.
   No chance for the briefest pause,
      unfortunate souls, no—
         we shrink and we tumble
         blindly from one hour
         to the next, water
           flung from precipice to
           precipice, perenni-
              ally down a deeper unknowing.

The Triangular Lodge

I

The Intercity passes it, so does the road
to Rushton. The fields nearby are striped
with taut electric tapes that tick. There is an odd

sensation of being at both the hub and the rim,
that something spinning fast speeds you ahead
while something else is still and shaded, firm.

God knocked three times. Sir Thomas Tresham's lodge
replies in triplicate. *That's three pounds twenty.*
The numbers click. *Enjoy.* Our binary age

may not quite understand the power of three:
here's two-way traffic, bright twin rails, the horses,
the bikes go by in pairs. But the trinity

hands over its receipt stamped *implications*,
and waiting for that third true line needs patience.

II

The monkey puzzles in the field have tried to count.
The rabbits multiply. Five five five five
above the door. TRES TESTIMONIUM DANT.

Three floors trefoiled and measured out in threes,
and Bible mottoes thirty-three letters long,
the seven lamps of fire, a lamb with seven eyes,

a dove, a pelican, a hand out of the sun
reaching to touch the Earth, a serpent wrapping
itself about a globe. Run, numbers, run

from your connegerie: in red and grey
courses your skins will hang and fetch three pounds
a hundred. Dappled by the Tudor day

and fit for contemplation—feeble things
compared with Him Whose glory this stone sings.

III

A rich man's folly: Prayer Book in the hedge
that Henry set, graffitied by a gamekeeper's
devices, soiled with droppings. On the verge

we're clueless, four-square, motor-mouthing types
whose bleak high rises are the true expression
of our soullessness. From these angelic pipes

that spout energy, mass, light, hear Tresham
dripping into immortality, his code
still not quite broken, and his brick equation

as unfathomable now as when Guy Fawkes
was found beneath the Commons plotting mass
murder: in that dark warren no one talks

and every word triangulates your guilt,
hung, drawn and quartered, so the lodge is built.

The Triangular Lodge in Northamptonshire (1593–1597) was Tresham's defiant celebration of the Catholicism for which he was imprisoned. 'Tres' refers to the Trinity ('There are three that give witness'), but was also the nickname his wife gave him. The building is full of such private allusions, number symbolism and allegory. My poem attempts a similar playful ambiguity. JG

Eglwys Llangwyfan

Surrounded at high tide, and still used
for worship during high season, the Church
in the Sea, where we stand congratulating

ourselves on one calm sunrise after Friday's
scourging breakers. These three have spelt
their names in clam and cockle on the rocky steps

that climb up to St Cwyfan's. They have
the old religion, but—to the oystercatchers' orange
warning *hwyl*—I feel the tug of an older

beneath eight centuries, beyond their shells,
that this stony path across the strand
leads west to, where a name in the turf

unnests a long-drowned Londoner.

Aberffraw, Anglesey

Thorney

for Stephen Hanvey

Finding myself in a forest of mast
and hoist, berth and cradle, the middle
of this boatyard, hoping to find
a footpath sign, I wonder how
after the station, after that bookshop,
we so quickly lost our way.

But past raw sewage, through flies
down a barbed and nettled tunnel—
now we see water, and it's clear
we're on the island, with a forbidden
wilderness fenced off in red:
KEEP OUT and UNEXPLODED.

A bright day. 'The Isle of Wight,'
you say, and there another friend
recedes like the tide. Defences
are crumbling everywhere, although
the Church of St Nicholas is still
standing ready for the next attack.

It watches over the graves of airmen
and over an open page of Domesday,
beyond the Great Deep. We keep
to the perimeter path, mud,
then shingle, sand, the sound of larks,
a microlight, and halyards tolling.

The Cathedral

Rilke: 'Die Kathedrale'

In such small cities, where the houses crouch
around on all sides, as if the hiring fair
had just that moment spotted it was there
and quickly shut up shop to stand and watch,

the racketing over, the thud-thud halted
as all ears strain in eagerness to attend—
while there it stands unflustered and enfolded
in the cloak of its flying buttresses, blind
to the very existence of these houses:

in such small cities, anyone may see
exactly how they have outgrown their closest
family, these cathedrals. Relentlessly
they rose above the rest—much as our own
view of life blocks out all other light
because we're far too close to see what's right,
as if there were no other show in town—
and what piled up in them might prove the rock
of fate itself, petrifaction that endures,
unlike here on the filthy street, where folk
accept whatever label fortune lures
them with, as kids grab clothing by the way
not knowing red from green because they're bored.
In these foundations, childbirth has occurred
and power rising through these stems has flowered
and bread and wine with love been shared each day
and porches echoed to each heartfelt chord.
Life heard the hours, but was not reassured:
high up among the towers there tolled the word
to reach no higher. Death had come to stay.

At Canterbury

I

The cathedral echoes with casual
remarks such as cost a king
his reputation. A toddler squeals

for sheer joy against the rage
of Henry the Second, the rage
of the German bombers, and ours

at forgetting our sandwich lunch.
We stand looking, and feel
mosaicked and grooved by the day.

II

First, sight advancing on a soliloquy
in black robes; up right, he stands near the steps.

Second, touch stretching out to discover
sackcloth and a horsehair vest. Thirdly, smell

smelling blood and inciting taste to take,
eat . . . Fifth is the sense I do not have.

For a Sixth, no sane man believes in it
until the day his brains go on a pilgrimage.

Fontevraud

Out of a forest more
silent than strictest vows,
through walls that once
confined a royal line,

to see Eleanor, with
Henry, Richard, and John's
queen, lying on stone,
untroubled by a twitter

of nesting from the cloisters
that raise serene white
eyebrows at something still
keen to escape the knot

of box hedging. Noon.
The world sends its chimes.
The abbey reaches out
to recover its lost hours.

Gradual

Arbroath Abbey

Half past two.

The Bell Rock Light
beats time
within the Old Round O

and my thoughts' chant is
of one sly tick

of hills beneath the tongue
of the warm seed rising
of tensile virtuosity
of a momentary wrenched escape

of vows
of long hugging laughter

of those arrows in a mighty hand

of a vine
of a strangulating vine

of an appeal
of an apologetic whimper
of emptiness
of post and the phone ringing

of footprints on the soft night stair

the refrigerating transept
the choir

Lift up your hands in the sanctuary
and bless the Lord

East Anglian Churches

They dance like paper cut-outs on a length of fishing line
across our windy county. The tail of a kite so high
it's almost out of sight, the cross of a man's agony

held by a child with his hands together on holy ground.
They dance—a tower, a spire; a porch, a flying buttress—
to the fantasia of an organ, to the thunder-repelling carillon

and they call to dance those who have forgotten what it means
to stop walking, stop running and skip, hop,
hornpipe to the music in the nave. If ever the wind drops,

what then? And already there is a change in the weather. One paper
cut-out is gone, another is torn, the kite itself is flying
erratically, the dance is uncertain, the music is played by old

arthritic fingers, there are bell-ropes hanging unused. Sing
your Shaker tunes, sing your Wesley anthems, sing, sing
hymns ancient and modern, for the child with his hands together,

for the children who will find the paper fragments littering the landscape,
make boats of them, make a treasure hunt of them, and not know
the secret in these crossed sticks, this fabric, the very wind.

from Huntingdonshire Nocturnes

Church Crawling

for Kevin Gardner

Leighton Bromswold

Yes, locked, of course. And once we find the key
it's comically huge, and hard to turn,
but when it does, George Herbert's century
comes tumbling, sliding, singing at my phone

from beams and dust and tracery and stone
as fresh-cut woodwork metaphysically
invites us to a pulpit. Choose which one.
For preaching of the Word? Or poetry?

Steeple Gidding

It's down a bumpy track, beside a field
of bumps, where a man and his manners failed.
The church is just an empty frontispiece,
though Cotton on the wall might help us trace

a web of stories to the primal source
of all our reading: whose library it was,
whose books became these tombstones, how the world
discovered learnedness must lose its hold.

Little Gidding

I often come. Not like a broken king,
more of a giddy pilgrim, remembering
the day I took that warm untroubled hand
there on the lawn at Ferrar House—profound

bubbling wapentake—before they could bring
his fame within the shaded panelling
of Herbert and Eliot, or call upon
Toomebridge to read the lesson. Lines from John.

Aldwincle

The prologue: here he was born. A smiling head
pokes out theatrically and shows us where
he entered. Next scene, All Saints: cross, admire
the stage-lit font they dipped him in, its lid

with hand-gel left there for the hand that's written,
'We're champing'. What? Until the plot's laid bare—
to camp in churches is the thing this year
of strange things. Epilogue: a plaque to Dryden.

Fotheringhay

Finally, this most final name. And yet
it hasn't finished. Something in the light
is darkening still. You move uncomfortably
as if you felt that fetterlock gyrate

up on the lantern. It's windless. At the great
absence of a fractal sky which might have set
the falcon free, it's what we cannot see
and can't return to. You must catch your flight.

On the last day of an October 2021 visit to the Greenings, I passed several memorable hours in pilgrimage with John, exploring churches along the Cambridgeshire–Northamptonshire border. At Leighton Bromswold, where Herbert held the living and installed the twin pulpits, we had to track down the keyholder to enter. The isolated and empty Steeple Gidding church bears a memorial to the Cotton family, whose most famous member was the antiquarian and collector of medieval manuscripts. Little Gidding awakened John's memories of meeting Seamus Heaney, their conversation interrupted by a summons to Heaney to read from the Gospel of John. John Dryden was born at Aldwincle rectory and baptized at the now redundant church across the road. Our journey ended at the magnificent but curiously truncated Fotheringhay, which revels in its unsettling associations with the Wars of the Roses and Mary Queen of Scots. John's title alludes to our mutual appreciation of the poet and tireless church crawler, John Betjeman. KG

Walking

One moment basking in the sun, the next knee-deep in snow
astonished at the way these tracks must have filled to the top
of their dry-stone walls during the April blizzards. To walk

has been the idea since we were small, and so we go on
along new paths and old, the way our parents led us,
listening for a curlew, looking at a weird extended ash,

checking our watches for the train, stopping for elevenses
among the sheep-droppings. It is a rhythm that we require,
that speaks of essences and immortality; not a pilgrimage

because there is no aim, the route is circular, but a stay
against age, climbing edge after edge, then out across
the moor above Eyam, that hostel you think you stayed in once.

Rex Tremendae

Walking alone up a lava flow
contemplating nothing, finding this
brings me closer to the truth than
organ music or even the Verdi
Requiem, which my father heard
before his death
                          hearing the piping
of a whimbrel trying to chase me
away from her nest, and seeing
the church spared by the eruption
from Krafla
                    perhaps I have found
what my father knew he meant
doing a Jimmy Stewart Glenn Miller
It's the sound . . .
                          It's the silence
of the King of Terrible Majesty
who is not Krafla

from Iceland Requiem

Offertorio

but life is not like the fjord at Akureyri
a beautiful dead end

                         something calls from its clear air
along the Arctic Circle down our Greenwich Mean
listening that is not the pips and the latest news
but like a golden plover of Idun or a loon's
ghostly warble across the water

                                 it is open for us
to hear if we will, through this dark mirror
of our mistakes

                      tune in, it asks, tune in
as men did once here separated from their homes
and their temperate ambitions by war

                              and hear
not the headlines, not the voice of a weather station
encoding the subterranean advances
of dark forces in their phallocentric depths

but the singing of offertories

                         whale song

                             seal cry

the corposant angels of St Elmo
escorting convoys with their gifts
and sirening their good news

                                  from Iceland Requiem

Cod

The fishermen are
gnostics in hooded
orange vestments

the sign of the fish
denotes the presence
of the absent

and empty nets
below the church
spell holiness

Lava

for Stuart Henson

It could have been a troll
or a glacier bookmark,
a puffin on a purse

or a key ring with Thor
swinging his hammer,
but I hit on this.

A spark from the Mývatn Fires
whose flow of lava
divided just in front

of the praying congregation
at Reykjahlið church
then smouldered five years.

I picked it as I climbed
towards the source
of this weird tale

up its long grey beard
towards an eye
that is still glittering.

Bunyan Meeting

After the Bunyan Museum—
where a stooping guide
followed me through clear
panels to talk of stained
glass, that famous image
Terry Waite received,
the only letter in all
his time in Lebanon,

where I examined the gaol
door and saw editions
abounding with his tinker's
anvil and metal violin,
and heard the steady drip
of faithful, hopeful talk
drown the shade of Bunyan's
oak-tree silence—I walked

through Bedford town centre
with my burden of purchases,
to find the bus home busy
discussing (as the gears groaned
from the Slough of Despond
up Hill Difficulty) the price
of drinks at Happy Hour
in the *Pilgrim's Progress*.

Nicholas Ferrar and the Pilgrim

'1592–1637. English theologian and mystic. An Anglican deacon, he founded a Utopian religious community at Little Gidding in Huntingdonshire (now Cambridgeshire).'

Chambers Biographical Dictionary

It is a gift—that you have journeyed here
to find me in my old life's final hours
at this cremation. These travel stories here
were futile dreams. I've learned to overhear
more useful omens as I sleep: this last
phantasma, for example, reached from here
towards a future time, on through the here-
after, where two were standing. One who prays
and one who never has. Therefore I praise
your stepping from that dream to greet me here
prepared to guide me through the fens of new-
fangleness, draining my path. You always knew

That this would be a gate to copses new,
beyond which certain instincts might cohere
and make it clear just what that avenue
of hamadryads whispered. Trees renew
themselves in special ways that could be ours,
in tree prayer, tree psalm, tree hymn. They start anew
each season, as we should. This is a new
testament deep within the heart, the last
unopened book of God. I have spent the last
ten years not seeing it, and now this new
light breaks across us both. Therefore I praise.
And yet there is a troubling truth that preys

On my ease. How could one who never prays,
whose life's a glistening web of all that's new,
a distraction-maze, a constant reapprais-
ing of romances, chances, fancies, praise-
less sneer, cold compliment, and a brief her-
oic moment, how could one such live praise-
worthily with our group where how it prays

is how it knows itself? And how, where hours
are spent in cheerful prayer and psalm as ours
have been, could one whose element is praise,
whose aim is at the spirit first and last,
how could that man survive, how even last

A single hour in your future? At last,
despite all this, we stand here and appraise
each other: who is the shoe, and who the last?
An owl cries in our silence. When I last
inspected I was Ferrar still, no new
appendages. The same fool. Made to last
like a horseshoe, to be hammered first, and last-
ly moulded for the grisly trot from here
to where our luck decides. So we stand here.
The children sang their psalm for me this last
few minutes: they know this smouldering hour's
a fuse, and soon I'll count by different hours

From those on their sundial. This now is ours
to weigh up. Treat each moment as your last,
we taught them. Savour the natural hours
beneath a stretch of blue we may call ours
before the sun goes when we'll have to praise
its honesty by moonshine. But to keep our-
selves under vague constellations, through hours
exposed to vast uncertainty, when new
dark pressures hold you down, when all you knew
is crushed into a hole of blackness—ours
is time's great challenge, and it's why we're here,
my friend, between the church and tomb, to hear

Our sentence read from all the writers' ashes here-
abouts, their motion purposeless as ours,
unable to distinguish first from last
as they drift to a judgement: let us praise,
if nothing more, all that we are, and knew.

from The Giddings

At Little Gidding

Caught in the space between Christmas and New Year, idly
wondering about Huntingdonshire churches: who uses them now?
Are we even closer to the fulfilling of Larkin's prophecy?

When the man in the four-by-four attempted to winch off
the lightning conductor from Little Staughton spire for the copper,
was that the beginning of the final act? Iconoclasts move

beyond stained glass and altar screens: they strike
at Michelangelo's very finger and bring down the roof. We snub
the churches around us and they ignore us back; though, on my bike

before Christmas, I reached Little Gidding and found the chapel
unlocked: not a soul, the community gone, a page
of signatures and Eliot on the wall; a bell, no steeple—

nothing for thieves or lightning. But something as shocking
struck me as I put on my cycle clips again and rode
home to wrap up your present—that book by Richard Dawkins.

from Huntingdonshire Elegies

Reversed Thunder

The Leighton hundred stone marks not the place
where Herbert preached, but the wapentake
of a barely Christian time. Here, lanes hold
their jaws wide as ever for a convenient
progress from missile base to carriageway:

that same hard shoulder I resorted to
a hundred terms ago, this pilgrim heart
heading through darkness to admit a mistake
and find its way home from something (the headlights
bear down, the ditch invites) not understood.

Epistle to St Guthlac

Old mate, we're nearly forty, why go on
squandering those few scraps still left to us
by feeding them to a fen of birds in Crowland?

Your wild beard thick with the shit of sea-fowl,
that silence you were forever longing for
unheard through all the quack, honk, hoot, hiss, boom.

I tell you, we were more intimate with peace
on Wessex fields, when blood-blessed, triumphant
and bodiless, souls sharp as blades, we stood—

all heaven in a vision, this life dust.
Just like that moral you'll now teach me, wiping
our past to nothing with a small soft word,

kneeling for hours in noisome sludge, for what?
To plough your strip of greed a hand's breadth more
in hopes of some inheritance beyond

this barrow you have chosen for your home,
the grave, you can be sure, of some crack fighter,
sword lying gold and white by his cracked cage?

Our final raid—how when we had kicked through
that stable, to a nest of angels, and after
one after another, remember, you said

you wished you could return their treasure to them,
they were entitled to one third . . . The birds
had got your brain, even then, and thus it came

and rose and burst and flooded all we knew.
Now there you pray, decaying like those rough skins
that stink upon you, a bestial ghost.

I have had bad dreams, old friend, about the sea,
a dragon that comes from the sea. So don't
tell me you've been taken to hell by demons.

Before he became a monk and a hermit out in the English Fen country, Guthlac (674–714) was a soldier in the army of Æthelred of Mercia. He founded Crowland Abbey where his cult flourished. JG

Nativity

One topic throughout the whole of Bethlehem tonight:
money—and the tyranny of Caesar Augustus.

But there are a variety of antidotes.

To mock the poor
(beggar, leper, lunatic)
who point and wildly cry
at the latest comet in the sky.

To hear your horoscope read by a wise man.

To run to the campfires
and dance and kiss through Saturnalia.

To enjoy a sly joke about King Herod.

Or, swaddled in cheap wine,
to follow the star of lust to its warm conclusion
in the straw of some unoccupied stall.

Angel, animal . . . impossible to distinguish.

Only that cry is recognisably shaped—
and then, the smirk of gold,
a shepherd's question mark,
the ingenuous slobber of a fatted calf
playing counterpoint
to the Christ child's first feed.

All believe, as yet, that they are here
to enjoy these riches:
this sweet and phosphorus manure,
the warmth, a mother's milk.

Magi

'I was a charming and respected teacher,
an influential man with everything
to lose by speaking out. I spoke. Now, who's
for Astro-Psychics class, Messiah Theory,
or Further Myth? This crock of frankincense
was my sardonic way (I'm famous for
those wry asides) of saying: well, yes, frankly
it's all nonsense.'
                        'In dreams . . .'
                                    'And may I add,
as world authority on processes
of mummification from the earliest
Dynastic to the Ptolemies it's good
to have escaped the lab, to sleep beneath
the stars—one hangs there so seductively
impelling us as if she's telling us
through wink and hint and dark suggestiveness
our necessary route—and see a way
that promises to bypass bodily
decay without the need for what I've brought
the child (wrapped here): embalming oils, the best
and purest treatment for mortality
humanity has yet—'
                        'For miles and miles
my only podium has been this hump.
And in it—all a beast requires. My friends,
we wanted more. Yet, far from your arcane
retorts and flasks, your glazed fork lightning, minds
made fit by study to confront the cosmos,
like me, do you begin to feel that you
have found some secret in this gentler sway,
that cloud-free sky, a sandscape of repeating
nursery dunes?'
                    'Let's rest.'
                                'In dreams, I reach
a shining building where the gold's not stacked
but scattered, so much of it that it's left

for goats or stuffed in scarecrows, valueless,
and all that's rare and longed for in that place
is wood, rough cross-beams, all their dreaming hung
with iron nails.'
                    'Can you feel this too, friends?
A wholeness, wholly blinding you to all
but one star, one clear scent out of the west?
It's growing dark. The desert ends beyond
that ridge, I'm sure of it. And if these moths
are not archangels, I'm . . . But I'm afraid
I have no dazzle left. An early class
tomorrow then, you magi, so good night.'

At Christmas

All easyJet flights
are cancelled—only
difficult journeys now.
Three in party hats
come dragging their presents
over a snowy car park.
A few attendants shepherd
them into a building:
the call to desert places.
Looking up for a moving
light or at Sky
News. Stasis over
the business empires.
A child has made an angel
by the automatic barrier
and a mother feeds her baby.
This breathtaking, breath-
making fall.

Christmas in Antarctica, 1911

Snowed up, 'snow on snow', we sing. Christina's
bleak winter can't have been a patch on ours.
If she could only have seen these
Three Foolish Men looking for their Emperor's
nesting place, she might have framed a more
sardonic sketch of faith: a penguin
messiah, a pilgrimage to the source
of ornithology, a flock of British bedouin
following a star called Scott, sanguine,
single file, in furs and silver, carrying instruments,
formaldehyde, and a box to put the eggs in.
The frosty wind made a moan like innocence
in agony, and the Selfridges display pane
was shattered by a jag of terminal moraine.

from The Winter Journey

Aubade

The sun's not up yet. There's still time
   to readjust the telescope
and pick out constellations, trace
a TV satellite through space
or watch the early planets climb
   to skim down morning's slope.

Insomnia is all it takes
   to reacquaint a working soul
with powers more than nine to five.
The fact that one is here, alive
and conscious, gradually wakes
   a force from some Black Hole.

Innumerable worlds roll by
   beyond this sealed-in window glass—
and each imagines it's unique
the way they lean a glowing cheek
with gravity upon the sky
   night-long. The lost suns pass,

but leave their light for those condemned
   to dark cells and the daily count.
No bail, no window, just one last
request before the cosmic blast
of Law—that, when we've done our time,
   these lenses on this mount

should point out into deeper space
   and show a simple truth go round
clear from the busy blur of here,
our light-polluted atmosphere,
this shrinking, shaking, turning place
   where every life is bound.

Pilgrims

for J

We're walking through the desert on the Nile's West Bank
to find St Simeon's Monastery, when suddenly our friend shouts
a snake! a snake! If it's a horned viper, he has minutes,
but decades later Miles is heading still for where we think
the sacred ruins are. A few hours. No one prayed.

Though in my head we're pilgrims. To walk for days, or even ride
as Frank did, on his bike to Santiago de Compostela
in answer to the call he heard from St James's scallop shell
out there at the end of the night sky's pearly road
in Finisterre. That's pilgrimage. Ours was a stroll with fate.

Nor was it Mecca. Nothing we'd want to celebrate
by painting our house with gaudy Boeings, and yet the sound of grains
rubbing against each other was a holy music, strains
of Speke and Burton, T. E. Lawrence, Captain Scott,
the search for a hidden source, the Pole. But also good to mock.

The Canterbury Pilgrims at least had a certainty to mark—
their turbulent feast. As you had when, that final day of summer,
you followed an unexpected longing to see them bring her home,
the lost princess. and off you went. Or when we flew to Knock
not for visions of Mary, but some visionary lines of Yeats.

Whereas at Walsingham we had been merely doing the sights
as someone touring our own shire might stop off to see
where prayer has been valid and hope (a fruitless hope) for tea
at Little Gidding. True pilgrims know that really it's
enough to make the journey once. Though nightly I set out

on wheels that take me down a preordained straight route
towards the spiritual, in sleep's weird mirage world
with friends I've never met and no familiar thing to hold
except our yellow water bottle—a badge that says doubt
everything but never doubt the sun will rise again.

Hieroglyphs

Westerners

we ferried our past across here
our furniture   our favourite things
the familiar parts of our life

we reconstructed them to make
ourselves an opulent future
and barricade oblivion

you will recognise us among
these everlasting earth treasures
in a gold mask   or in black granite

in the clean slot of a hieroglyphic
though you thought we were dead and strange
you will recognise us   we are

still here   we are the westerners

Crossing

between haunches
baskets full of aubergine

the mothers

they rest their heads
their sickly bundles
on my shoes
or on my wife's thigh

the mothers
they surround us

hardly moving

a drum
hollow

muttering
bismillah!

hardly a breath

the ferry man
perhaps the father of a handful

though from the ditches in his face
the father
of a million
every year

fixes his narrow gaze on the bend
from which the breeze will come

we contemplate
a childless sky

and half a mile
of freedom

The Wife of Nakht-Min

His fat hands waggle, the policeman laughs,
and the loafing attendant licks the feather-duster handle.
All grease the glass with their noses, all pass the case
and take a snap. But some glance a second longer.

Her face, mutilated for reasons we don't know,
is still sufficiently fine to make us wonder
what else she hid behind the huge coiffure
fastened there like a cask of wine four thousand years.

Though the eyes and the lips have been destroyed
and a carved gold band is clamping the skull
so the plaited and tressed triumphal pylons
chain her in hair from head to chest,

she can still gaze and smile undamaged
through the small favours her sculptor bestowed:
a lotus flower opening under claw-tight buds,
pomegranates tucked beneath a barren strip of gold,

how the sheaved and stately queen comes firm and small
into a ripe young girl where the corkscrew curls run out,
how the severed hand that should have reached towards the king's son,
though severed, still clutches at some carved frippery,

and how an inspiration—the film of pleated
fine linen—ripples through indurated stone
to reveal the shapely abdomen and nubile curves
light, below the weight of a wifely crown.

> *my lover*
> *I like to go to the lake with you*
> *and wash there*
> *allowing you to see me*
> *wet*
> *in my linen gown*
> *of pure white*

Sweet Morning Tea

The fan smiles
and shakes its head consolingly—

that fierce blue gaze
that withering yellow tongue—
this afternoon is inconsolable!

As evening
when the fan is sleeping
and she's allowed out veiled
I have found she's a cool companion

but as night
in star-dropped nakedness
then the questions wink:

Why did you ever leave your home
when everything
your everything
and everything you are is there?

Perhaps you couldn't appreciate
through all those domestic stirrings
all those teacup storms
the excellence of the white bone china.

Perhaps you will
when your cool companion
in her tomorrow dress
brings you her sweet morning tea

and the glass burns you
and the drink is black, without milk.

Coptic

for Kevin Gardner

And so they come knocking at
our falseness, inviting us
to befriend and to condemn.

.

Have we seen the island, where
Joseph's famine is inscribed?
The fish cools on the table.

.

A storm gathering. Killings
downriver, a Pope exiled,
and their lost inheritance.

.

We'd talk all night about Wright's
Coal Tar and of the many
ways the West knows how to clean.

.

Faces turning sideways through
endless television to
look at us from their tomb walls.

.

One keeps declaring his love
for Christ and any Western
woman who believes in him.

.

These two run a trinket shop:
each ankh, a cross with a knot,
is a gift of the dammed Nile.

.

For Christmas, she held a duck's
neck over an empty can
of sunflower oil and slit it.

                    .

While other shuffling cantors
on the balcony haven't
guessed yet they're not hieroglyphs.

                    .

Just some stones, he sighs, as we
reach the open mouths of those
he proudly called ancestors.

                    .

The ceremony was a
long slow royal barge journey,
driven by a living word.

                    .

And truly they consider
they are heirs to the riches
laid here—of language, spirit.

                    .

(When I spoke of all this, years
later, what came back was dead-
pan English: *Copts and Robbers*.)

The Crack

The Pharaoh has arrived in Aswan today:
being cheered off the barge, being greeted
by officials from the quarry, on his way

through the streets, luxuriously seated
in a palanquin, to supervise the long-planned
raising up of his newly completed

obelisk. Across desert, up the grand
triumphal causeway carved for this occasion,
he's escorted to where the workmen stand,

their faces smooth, as if the abrasion
of a fear, of a persistent nightmare,
had ground them away. Without expression,

they watch their foreman whisper in an ear
and the quarry official gasp, fall dumb
and helpless and leave the foreman to steer

the guest away. He knows the worst must come,
but he can patch time, pointing out the vast
unyielding rock face and outlining some

of the problems caused by having to work fast
and make crucial cuts too quickly, with risk
of ruin . . . Leading the falcon eye past

the hollow of a previous obelisk
which only the rock's good temper had meant
it was finished and erected in weeks . . .

But the Pharaoh has begun his ascent:
lifted over the rock these men wrestled
to overthrow, shaded from rays they spent

long months exposed to—some of them pressing
the wooden wedges in the hard-worked slots
and dampening them to swell, some dressing

the hacked-out shape for the final cuts—
and all, even through the pink rock dust, pale
as alabaster now, aware of what's

made out to quarry employees who fail
to finish their allotted task before
the Pharaoh comes. Today, it's a fairy tale.

But that day it was as if the earth's core
had pumped a deep black vein of evil up
out through the granite slab, and the men saw

the crack, as if they were watching a heart stop.

Ozymandias Revisited

The wrinkled lip has reverted to pink
granite, the features to igneous flecks:
no passions or pedestal. You can't think
such rubble was a king once, that his legs
and loins there, unstirring now in the gorse
were firm as the phallic pillars. Here, two
neat hands on knees, then the broken torso
distorted, heaped like a mass grave. A son grew
as tall as him perhaps, and whipped a purge
that toppled him? No, none. Only the ur-
force, time, can have erased a demiurge
utterly. Now it's only on the tour
so the guide can quote with outstretched hand
'I met a traveller from an antique land . . .'

Nefertiti in the North

Not to be closer
to the roots
of this rose

in lands
where they say the Nile
no longer flows

but falls
like the sunlight

not to be watching
the bird-catchers
crouch
where the gardens end
outside my window

and that same figure
on my wall

not for the paintings
of his nets and his dog
driving from the papyrus thickets
a slim-necked waterfowl

not for these

and not to be quenched
by the sight
of the sand's disregard
for his sacred boundaries

never to scoff in triumph

'the-beautiful-woman-has-come'
has come

but since the King
is in the south
in the company
of his dear Smenkhare

I have come
to this castle in the north

The Amarna Stelae

At Karnak, who was it unearthed
in nineteen twenty-five
those twenty-five colossi
of Akhenaten? In the photograph
they rise up out of the sand
like science-fiction clones
or giant ivory chessmen
dropped at the end of a game
on a beach in the Hebrides.

They are caricatures of what
these twenty-five years
have made of one who stood
arms folded and holding
a flail to palely control
a class of Egyptian girls.
After me. What's your name?
Mr John, Mr John,
where you get pot belly?

Too much of Egypt has gone
to try and reconstruct
determinatives. Look at this
album with half its photos
fallen out, odd inscriptions
above blurred faces; at our
spoilheap of slides and this
ciné we cannot translate
into any blank cartouche.

Voices that cheered the First
Cataract with us or sang us
to Kitchener's Island have fallen
dumb, have dried at their source
to the fixed mummy-smiles
of Tjuyu and Yuya, a mother

and father, her hair plaited,
his mouth opening. My parents
have stopped singing, too.

At the Colossi on the West Bank
where we leaned our hired bikes
and Dad's *ka* went out
of control for lack of sugar
(sugar stirring all about us),
lumps of crumbling figure
guard a temple that has gone,
though a spirit free-wheeled there,
Akhenaten's gold begetter.

Was it love or self that drove us
to escape high priests and viziers,
to find a freer style for our
marriage in that bow of the Nile,
an aim fletched with the Truth
Feather, to penetrate the Window
of Appearance? Glass shimmering
between us. The Priests of Money
putting paid to the experiment.

The Hidden One proclaims
Akhenaten's move was politic,
the sun he worshipped was himself,
his Venusian features, woman's
pelvis, spindly limbs,
curved spine, bent
knees were caused by a disease
which made him blind and led
to such touching scenes of intimacy

with Nefertiti, who was never
exiled to that 'castle in the north'
but changed her name, her sex,
became co-regent, left
posterity and Hitler the face

she wished to show, turning
a blind eye as the wall
came down, and mocking
all other women.

Checkmate. The king is dead.
These stelae mark his boundaries.
We live on as minimalists
dreaming a Tutankhamun
might clear our title to a castle
or fix the roof. Our daughters
breathe the western wind—
but one has asked for a scarab
and one is a worshipper of the sun.

The Treasures of Tutankhamun

The British Museum, 1972

I am waiting, like all the others, waiting
to open the sacred seal and discover
my future; and as I wait, this exhibition
snakes me through steel barriers to my golden
eighteenth year where I catch, amid the darkness
that enfolds a teenage pharaoh's history,

glimmerings of a more personal history,
as if it had lain beneath the sand waiting
for me to come and dig into its darkness
in search of the famous mask but discover
only in each glass case my own face, golden.
It is my coming-of-age exhibition.

All aspects of me are in this exhibition:
the child's chair and board game are a history
of my early youth; my teens were that golden
dagger. This trumpet, this cow-bed are waiting
for me to experiment, to discover
in their cross-meshed passages of darkness,

in sexual unity and divine darkness,
the Goddess Hathor's milk-white exhibition
of her transfiguring powers: discover
between her lyriform horns all history.
The Necklace of the Rising Sun is waiting
to embrace us, its clasp is cool and golden . . .

Each morning my hopes shoot greener, but golden
futures only bloom after months in darkness,
during nights of counting the weeks of waiting,
and now at this jubilee exhibition
I am persuaded that time and history
are relative. Come, UCCA! and discover

to me the sacred light, let us discover
the place where we are to spend our golden
prime and inscribe our names on history
as one young man did, emerging from darkness
at eighteen to become this exhibition—
the very thing for which we are all waiting.

For "UCCA," see An Interview with John Greening, p. 429. KG

For My Father

March, 1923: now the sealed door
is opened in the Valley of the Tombs
of the Kings; and in Chiswick, you are born—
not to a blaze of flash photography,
but crawling the width of a no-man's-land
between two wars. Nor will you be brought up
like a king, but by the time you are eighteen
know the riches of possessing a bike
and wireless. No time for ancient history.
When you join up, you are delivered into
a modern, disarmingly naïve land,
so new it still bubbles. In Akureyri,
your headset is picking up hieroglyphs,
but nothing, no greeting, from The Black Land
or Living-Image-of-the-Hidden-One,
that eighteen-year-old with whom you share
a birthday; and it will be forty years
before you feel you can make contact with
your contemporary.

                    But by the time
we were pedalling into El Gurnah (famous
for its bandits) past squatting black covens
of women, their sons like huge weathered masts
white lateen-sailed, your 7 a.m. breakfast
had risen to 12 noon, and we panicked
because of your diabetes. Semi-
conscious, slumped there beside a drainage ditch
in a field of sugar, the sugar carts
swishing past, unrefined wallads flicking
the flies away and chewing lengths of cane,
you had regressed to the nineteen-twenties:
when (from that tomb-robbing Gurnah clan) down
came a stranger, who climbed out of his taxi
and silently removed you to his house,
no rock chamber in the foothills, no cache
of Middle Kingdom murals, but a simple

whitewashed tunnel-vaulted house of mud brick
there on the fertile plain. Nor was his wife
laden with stolen pharaonic jewellery,
but brought us refreshing hibiscus juice,
and led you to lie beneath the cool vault
of an empty bedroom.

                    Apart from the curse
of disease, I don't believe in curses:
although it was you who first directed me
to the dog that died, the lights that failed,
and Weigall's prophetic, 'Well, if he goes
down the tomb in that spirit, I give him
six weeks to live!' But I do remember
that your recovery seemed miraculous,
and when, the day after, you felt quite able
to walk down those sixteen steps, sixty years
of Tutankhamun seemed inconsequential.

The Cedars at Highclere

I see him in the distance. The stories he tells them
waft across to me as I trim the lawns beneath his cedars.

He loves cedars: his father asked my father to put them in.
The Egyptians made all their tables and chairs out of cedar,

he told me once, were buried surrounded by it. Now he's
alone on that fancy verandah, reading, or glancing up towards

these living crowns—always some fat volume open beside him.
That's (he'd say) since forty days stuck out in tropical seas

with so little to do, between fighting off pirates
and avoiding hurricanes, he fell prey to the bookworm.

But we know. In the old days he would never have stopped
still long enough to have turned a leaf. If it wasn't the sea,

it was the turf; if it wasn't the latest horseless carriage,
it was some infernal air machine. Faster, always faster, until

Trotman comes running to pluck him out from that blazing wreck
in the Black Forest—head smashed, heart stopped.

And all he wanted to know was had he killed anybody.
Next thing, he is making Highclere a home for war-wounded,

young lads cowering behind this shadow-line: muttering, wide-eyed
ghost battalions. M'lord was never one to let the grass grow.

Today he showed us another of his latest photographs—one of
a mummified cat, which wasn't at all well received by his dog,

nor by her Ladyship, for that matter. But then, we all have doubts
about this digging up of times long gone. The papers make jokes

about the thousands he has wasted (with 36,000 acres
here to keep) and to my own thinking, when there's talk of a curse

you think twice. He's already had a good nine lives—chased
by a wild elephant in South Africa (more of an achievement

to have escaped than shot it, he said), then only last week
rushed to the hospital with three quarters of an hour to live.

When he dies, it will be in a way nobody could have foreseen.
'I don't think I've lost my nerve,' he whispered, straight

after that accident. And he won't let anyone wrap him up
in bandages. 'I want to be buried,' he laughs, 'out in the open,

high up on Beacon Hill, then if you like—' to us, he calls us
his garden angels—'plant one of de Havilland's DH9s

above me like a pyramid; and make sure the grave is dug
by a professional archaeologist!' Tomorrow he's off out

to the East again. The last season, he has announced.
'If the pharaohs don't bite, the mosquitoes certainly will.'

Carter at Swaffham

We know him: it's
the Carter lad who
painted dear Lady
Amherst's lapdog

and the Vicar's old
bull terrier, quite
without schooling—son
of our gamekeeper's son.

And if his imagination
pierces a tiny hole
in these venerable walls
and holds a candle

through to a room full
of wonderful things
but utterly foreign to
a decorously mounted

hunting party with
its fine equipage,
its whips and sticks and
stuccoed wooden courtesy—

then what is that to us?
Tally-ho! and on towards
the twentieth century: let
the boy be content

with keeping trespassers
from our noble pile;
or immortalise our
ailing Golden Retrievers.

Carter Begins

I

There is a language of rock that is not
like the language of diplomacy

or newspapers or love. One must know
how to read it, where to begin. None of us

has heard it spoken, though some taste the air
into which its last words evaporated,

a few have grovelled to wrench gold fillings
from its mouth. There is a grammar of rock,

but its secrets are guarded by aloof
priestesses, their fingers to their lips as they

scald meaning from the bones. I will begin
with a triangle I know to mean hope.

Aboard the *Champollion*, steaming
towards the Pharos, unknown, unrecognised,

I imagine steps that lead into chambers
full of the poetry of this rock language.

II

The Valley in which we search
fruitlessly is peaceful:

we dream of gardens or of
a golden age, and our looking

is contented. If we knew what
sentences of hard labour

await us the day we crack
the dream, we would not know

this pleasure, sipping at
perhaps and may, shifting

ten thousand irritations
at a stroke. But the demons

of discovery are less
considerate—they will block-

book the hotels, and arrive
each morning in dark glasses,

rattling metal plates,
begging their thousand words.

III

Down to bedrock now—but
all we have to show is

thirteen jars containing
the remains of sweet oils

used to anoint the dead.
Lady Carnarvon stoops

and for an instant glows
Pre-Raphaelite again:

Miss Almina Wombwell
delivering the first

flush of her youth into
her lover's arms. Is this

a final remembrance
of 'that night devoted

to oils, when thou art re-
united with the earth'?

Now she kneels to a lost
fragrance, alabaster

jars look pale disciples;
and we—two wretched thieves

mocked and left here to parch
with a mystery king.

Carter's Descent

February 1924

To come down these sixteen steps
holding the keys, the sole keys,
and hearing the reverberation from
that heavy iron grille; to know
that not even the *Times* correspondent
can follow me here . . .
                              To come down
and enter the darkness and to see
through the darkness a cracked lid
still suspended above that
most public, most secret mask, not
shaped to reflect either the lunacy
of a heretic predecessor or a star-
blind sacerdotage, but to glow
below the horizon of the sun-disc
modestly—no papyri, no press . . .

To come down where everyone has appeared
to understand why their hands must be tied,
their heads bowed, their tongues slit—
why everything (chariot, ostrich feather
fan, mere child's toy) must be restrung
along my endless, exact, but unbreakable lines . . .

To come down where I have felt
alive and in command as if
it had been my own kingdom and I
liberated from fake courtesies
(permission denied/permission granted),
gilded wooden minds, hollow talkers . . .

To come down and handle a reed basket
of three thousand years ago, and forget
the three thousand unanswered letters
in my identical basket—
                              Surely you must be
our long lost cousin from Camberwell . . . ?
Might this perhaps cast light on the crisis
in the Congo . . . ? Just send me a gold bar
or two—some mummy cloth—some of the beer
dregs—a grain of sand—I enclose half
a crown . . .
                    To come down
to where the responsibility and the doubt
do not hang on their frayed ropes
like halves of that granite lid
cracked by a priest's men in antiquity,
lifted through the power of the English aristocracy,
abandoned to a rotten Egyptian bureaucracy . . .

Carnarvon—you would have smiled,
you would have gone out and shot a few hundred
rabbits or opened a magnum and toasted one
of two kings, or rested on this barbaric couch
before hurrying down to your beloved darkroom . . .

Carnarvon—your dog, your favourite dog,
howled and died with all the lights of Cairo
that April morning . . .
but the high, clear air of Beacon Hill
was golden, as they buried you, with lark song.

At noon, under the desert sun, I discover
steps that lead deep into myself.

To come down to this dark
and to know that after the long

bolero brays its climax
and the final veil of bullion
has been lifted, there will be sudden
leather and tooth and rag,
and the same bejewelled ignorance
as when we began—
                              is to come down
to earth, is to come down
to brass tacks, is to come down
carrying heavy iron keys
and to leave with a glimpse
of the golden ankh.

Lifting the Lid

Lifting the lid on our
uncertain longing
for a god—

these ropes and pulleys
are the liturgy
of modern belief,

but no explanation of
darkness can
be found in the light—

when you touch your
own hand in the mirror,
what you feel is glass.

The Day I Found King Tut

Opposite the British Museum
just along from Coptic Street
is Davenports,
the magicians' shop.

I used to get their catalogue
sent and crept nightly
into the treasury:
fans, flowers, Floating

Zombies, Find the Lady,
Funny Bunny, Indian
Rope Trick, Chinese Rings—
and on the back page

all I could afford,
the after-dinner jokes:
a blue plastic coffin
with a red plastic

'King Tut' lying
quite snugly, held
by a concealed magnet,
which, with a sleight

of hand, you could
dislodge so that
like-poles repelled
and the Pharaoh would

not lie down, would
not lie down, only
you the arrogant
thirteen-year-old

knew how! I was
a regular mummy's
curse from the day
I found King Tut.

Of Paradise

An oriole on the islands of the First Cataract.
An osprey in the Nile as I cross on a felucca.
The egrets, white shadows of the sacred ibis.
The hoopoes, exotic moths of the midday flame.

And on the West Bank where the dead make nests
and the Nubians have been made to live in dovecotes,
a bird-catcher from one of the Nobles' Tombs
crouches with his long net, to dam the skies.

Omm Sety's Farewell

We
were packing all our souvenirs and gifts
for the flight back home
when you set out on your voyage to Amenti,
Omm Sety. We had stayed
two years, our poorest and our richest,
you—half a century
of intercourse across thirty centuries.
Scent or strain of music,
gesture, profile, touch,
that last glance back—
like paintings in the Tomb of
the Remainder of our Lives, just one
false door, marked
POETRY, to allow the *ka*
to come and go as now
it does, remembering that day
in 'eighty-one, when—
did we even hear about it? We were too busy
arranging who would take our cat, a note
in our diary says she was very nervous, it was
'an odd evening'. We said goodbye to our friends
resting our eyes again on the West Bank.

Leave your cats, your Teti-Sheri,
your Hor-em-heb: on this last ferry
no Ramesses, Ankhsi, Ahmes, Mery.
Your animals will sing to you.
Leave your gander, leave your goose.
Snofru, Nebet, set them loose.
You need no watch on your new house.
Your animals will sing to you.
Leave your rabbit, leave your dog
Khalouli. Surely leave that frog
called Pharaoh to his monologue.
Your animals will sing to you.

Leave your birds, your peregrine.
Like these vipers, shed your skin.
My horse Mut-ho-tep calls you in.
Your animals all sing to you.

                We
    who love her, find a mysterious life
            in Abydos: other ears
than mine have heard the music in the halls,
        the sistrum, tambourine and pipe.
    And other eyes have seen the golden glow
            in the Sanctuary of Osiris
    when no lamp was lit. And I have stood
            alone in Pega-the-gap
            at the Great Feast of Osiris
            listening to the jackals howl
            but at midnight, immediately
            the jackals were hushed, a deep
            silence fell and I
            felt myself surrounded
            by a great multitude of people,
            heard their breath, their feet
            on the sand, and as I passed
    through the gates of the Temple of Osiris,
    their presence, their breathing, their whispering feet
    vanished into the past, and I was left
    with only the stars and the cold of ruined
    walls, their clear impenetrable text.

Mr Stuart in Aswan

for the Revd Stuart Evans

We stepped out on thin ice, then back, without
blinking an eye. It was a dream, I'm sure,
those two years married up the Nile, so hot
and poor, so hard on lovers. Sky is pure
lazulite today, our thermometer
reads minus and the lawn is wreathed in white:
a flickering cartouche 'has this report . . .'

But you are back there, where Pythagorean
sails still catch the pharaohs' breath and Nile
keeps peace with Kitchener, the Aga Khan's
white dome with iron hills. Our life here pales
beside it all, a fertile strip that peels
to western desert, tired tracks of a viper,
a quarter century's markings undeciphered.

Walk down the souk for me, old friend, and fill
a genie bottle with that dried date scent:
then mix some cumin and some guava smells
with howling feedback from a muezzin,
squeeze in a lemon seller's grin, the glint
of coffee brass, or tea glass, black, sweet, kohl
and jasmine, a displaced Nubian smile.

I'll risk the evil eye, unsilt that door
darkening tomb wall paintings, the High Dam
extinguishing light to show its power.
No fertile inundation will now come—
and Isis only in this broken dream
of walking the white lake: a dark cortege
that works its silent way across my page.

The Temple of Isis

for Alan Bolesworth

Magic! Alan would say, if Jane
produced a tray of basbousa
rich in sugary syrup and semolina,

or managed to conjure Christmas pudding
out of nothing but twenty-seven varieties
of date and a few weevils. *Magic!*

And the travellers come to visit us
like Magi in January (wisely), bringing
their gifts of instant coffee granules,

teabags and Fairy Liquid,
and we will escort them to the High Dam,
to Philae, to the Temple of Isis (saved

by modern technology from the Flood) and fix
in bright relief the black arts
no camera can expose: a Nubian crone

blindly rowing them between cataracts,
a *fellah* preserving his wrinkles against
the evil eye, the kids with their trachoma

and their stones, 'PEACE' above arms cradling
illiteracy and death. Then—magic!
Isis rising on her reconstructed pylons

to remind us of Osiris, of the surgery she performed . . .
Only to sink back, her power drained
into a new power, for the processing of sugar.

The Scarab Cake

Our daughter's chosen birthday cake's
a scarab: she's been studying
Egyptians. Here, among my books
the lapis lazuli is hidden,
its icing hard and blue, its sun
a chocolate orange rolling on

into her teens. This scarab seal
was Khepri or 'He Who Becomes',
whose little dung ball used to roll
down obelisks, papyri, tombs,
but finished up with souvenirs
that westerners hang from their ears

at birthday parties. Rosie's ten,
and that seems like a dynasty
to her. But think back twenty, when
we lived in Egypt—then, how we
ruled our Old Kingdom! All that waste
collected, shaped, and dribbled west

on camel spoors, until we found
this campsite. Scarabs symbolise
the dawn of hope of dawn, how ground
can breed new stars, and tantalise
us into thinking it's not wrong
to spend a lifetime pushing dung.

The roller-skating party's over:
at last, the scarab cake appears,
its candles lit, its sun-disc shivered
to moon pieces. How many years
have we done this? Sing. Take the knife.
And share the sweets of future life.

Bubastis

The cat sleeps all night and goes out hunting by day,
the way we have trained her to. Now she brings back
shrews and butterflies and song thrushes for us to admire.

Ziggy we call her, short for Zagazig—the place
where there's a City of the Dead for cats: Bubastis. Sacred
to the cat goddess, Bastet. Our little Bastet

is watching that blackbird, dreaming she is Sekhmet,
the Destroyer. She stalks its tone rows patiently. Dreams of it
in thirteen different ways. As the dark makes velvet paws

we sing for her: *Zigpuss! Ziggy! Zig!Zig!Zig!*

from Huntingdonshire Nocturnes

There Is a Garden

There is a garden in the next world
where all the birds and fish and plants
that we have exterminated are being kept—

I think it is this seedbank that I visit
occasionally when I am sleeping and wake
to feel as if some part of me has gone out

and spent the night travelling, as Egyptians
used to believe and so would leave a false
door out of their tombs. Within that garden

which I imagine to be like the one at Kew
where my parents lived and where I was born
and taken through the penny turnstile

and in which there is no perspective, fish and ducks
lying sideways against the surface of the pool,
trees unfolded flat from its edges, yet where all

comes into a true angle because the light
is the light that was in Egypt when we were there,
the fragmentation of the tomb will hardly matter.

This will be enough: just as a speck of DNA
can reconstruct the scene, the life, I am hoping
that in this garden there is somewhere that I can learn

to plant and grow things as I never let myself
be taught by my father or to pave a proper path
as I watched my mother do. There will be fruits there—

I can see them in this last surviving scene, the dates,
the figs, the ghastly doum. But also grapes. And some papyrus
for writing on too, if in that garden writing is allowed.

Home

The Scene of the Fire

Rilke: 'Die Brandstätte'

The early autumn day, cautious, would rather
avoid it, but where those frazzled lime trees grew
close to the cottage wall there was a new,
an empty something. Here would be another

spot for screaming children (and God knows where their
parents are) to come and fight in, grabbing scraps.
But all of them fell quiet when they saw the
son who'd lived there heave from the collapsed

half-burned-out timbers, still hot, a distorted
kettle or an old copper, with a long
forked branch, and looking as though he'd been caught
in a lie, stare at them, in case they doubted

the truth of what he'd seen and knew had perished.
That this could even not be here still seemed
to him as strange as something Pharaoh dreamed.
And he was changed. A foreigner, a tourist.

Suburbs

Eastcote, Middlesex, 1982

On the suburban moor
net curtains hang like mist,
the terrain is grey with hibernation
and the same thinning growth.

As you pass, a hand hovers in the window,
its invisible eye colouring you in,
the chirring of a lawnmower breaks off . . .

Behind these comfortably green hedges
is an acidic bog, preserving
ancient forests of grudge:

one foot wrong, and all eyes will bubble up
and with a smiling, slurping—*he. . . ? No!*
suck you down into the slander.

Under the Flight Path

My entrance is a cul-de-sac off Hounslow Heath,
once feared for masked hold-ups, an airport now,
characterless; but in that ambrosial flask

are sealed these precious vagrants on a patch
of mid-century. Britannias above them
feathering home, Tridents puncturing

extended conversation like a banjo skin—
and in the memory, the head's resonating
membrane, string still answers string . . .

Here, 'King Spring' rolls out of his sleek taxi,
home to his mint Great Britain collection,
his Mahler boxed sets; and his Persian wife,

who loves her cockatoo, takes in stray cats,
and will leave him for a mongrel, knocks
and keeps knocking at our door for sugar;

while, through our party wall, 'The Peasants',
hammer and tongues, young newlyweds (who outside
speak softly of fishing and babies) spit fire;

as 'Boudicca', next door but one, crashes back
in her Anglia, ticket equipment slung at her breast,
from battle on the Bath Road's bloody buses.

Or as, along my secret cinder-and-ash backway,
the Crops' son carries his cleft palate,
deaf smile, and a box (for me) full of Superman;

past Old Man Withinshaw, who'd shout as I picked
pale and skeletal lanterns near his chicken run,
whose granddaughter looks out from her leukaemia,

Going to see Lord Jesus . . . Next door, the teacher's
daughter knows Paul McCartney; next door, the surgeon
is flying Tim and Toot to South Africa; next door,

the Major's son has been given permission to ride
a motor scooter, and shows me his home-made rifle,
and cowboys every midnight below my window,

plucking love on the banjo's neck. There's Elaine,
my pal from primary school, all at once
blonde, leggy and my pal no more. And there's

Sally, limping down the ash-and-cinder alley,
one leg too long, leaning into her viola case
and lisping to the Great West Road. Other,

mysterious, neighbours also: the brothers
on the corner, their high-walled garden,
shy nocturnals. And gay birds like the Kellys,

ever flitting off to Heathrow pyjama parties,
free passes to the world's airspace. And once,
they flew me in their Morris Minor to Littlehampton.

Does Concorde still shiver my bedroom? Is Eve there
trilling a war song on her lawn to intercept it
above our air-raid shelter? Next-door-but-

twenty-odd-years, who are those furred and haughty,
horn-rimmed and raincoated, unspeaking caricatures?
The Brittens: they keep chained a cartoon bulldog

and are pure Aryan. But it's old Mr Mortimer
and old Mr Wheeler, double-digging the trenched
alluvium of their days, who speak the silence

gone with orchard, heath and pond; and one of them
was visited one day by a crew-cut American boy
I wanted to impress with my Gemini bike act:

seeing the door is closed, instead I hurry home
with my prize astronomy project, like a genie
aborting take-off, dropping back into the bottle.

Clinton, New Jersey

Sim Free

It was a shiny moulded beehive,
something of my mother's perhaps,
to do with knitting. In my sticky hands
it became a pretend camera

and in its green bakelite brain
from nineteen sixty-two or -three
all my childhood days are stored,
if only we could find the thing

and wake it. But the technology
of I'll be this and you be that
and here is there has gone away
somewhere, inaccessible, play-

time over. I've lost the knack
of clicking into that imaginary
zone, of being whatever I wanted
at shutter-speed. Sweet dreams.

Kew

What am I trying to
get into with this one
old penny?

        the turnstile
clicks satisfyingly
its glossy black coldness
lets me through

        the turnstile
moves just one way, admits
only one memory
at a time

        the turnstile
opens its prison bars
on to my first year at
Kew Gardens

        the turnstile
still turns, my penny rests
on that eye of the dead

There is no queue. To leave
it costs nothing. Just push
the turnstile

      you are tired
but though your legs won't work
no pushchair can pass through
the turnstile

      this Easter
we have been revived by
what can be seen beyond
the turnstile

      but where is
Grandpa? Where is Auntie
Daisy? Haven't I grown . . .

the turnstile
groans its own reply. No
Admittance After Dusk.

The Thames

A river that has coiled about me
like desire: I climbed the very
terraces to school each day,
divined its presence, knew
its power, that it was glimpsed
from Green Lines to Windsor
Great Park, and spotted
on Red Rovers to Battersea
funfair, that it ruled Richmond
and Twickenham and smelt out
Brentford, Isleworth, Hounslow,
that it was near home.
                          My father
like me, Thames-born, dug
the prime alluvial soil
and quoted bits of *Three Men
in a Boat*, and twice we
took one out for the day
from Sunbury, *Beau Geste*
the name I unreeled over
into dark eddies, imagining
a pike or rainbow perch
and catching rudd.
                          There were
stories: a constant wash
of quicksands and drownings, of one
who fell from his boat and caught
Green Monkey Disease, of one
who left his clothes folded
neatly on the bank, of fish
vanishing and fish returning,
of a dolphin at Tower Bridge,
of the coming barrage, of a small
god or a jewelled sword-hilt

salvaged, of a child my age
dragged clear.
            My youth
walks the towpath, looking
up at a tall chimney, grand
Palladian villas, shapely
bridges, feeding the swans
that Spenser knew unknowing
how rich the fare, but towed
by a Friday grandfather
from his Defoe Avenue home:
a castaway I, aware that
the river could rise and flood
childhood coral as it had in
those sepia photographs—fear
of wet sandbags mingling
with Grandpa's home-grown
tobacco hung up to dry
like seaweed in the chequered
sea-cave of his kitchen, an old
black magnet on his shelf,
an iron mae west that so
attracts me I clutch at it
and he shouts to me 'Don't—'
through the gas-fire roar
of surf on rocks.
            At Kew,
everything started opening:
gardens that seemed the river's
child, the heart of desire,
Eden where I hyperventilate
still under oxygenating glass,
palm, alpine, monkey puzzle,
sacrarium of conkers, open
prospects and a shut pagoda—
at Kew I am first hugged, then

crushed by the dragon Thames,
for she runs through everything
those days: they are a meadow
in my past that, now it is
swept by water, blooms
with orchids.
                    We married in
a meander of the Thames, lived
in an oxbow, and walked
Waterloo Bridge mornings
at ten to the hour, below us
its broad black threat
of homelessness. You'd lived
in Hampton; I in Hounslow
had been drawn across
the dry conceptual heath
to your soft waters,
to the maze and stately home,
to the locks of my childhood . . .

The earliest memory I own
is of something dimly bright,
warmly frightening at Boulters
Lock—some bold confession
by the old gathered there
for a last day out, or
the moment of my own wakening:
I too will grow up
and grow old?
                    It took
the Nile to loose the river's
world serpent grasp
on our lives.
                    Our love
a long walk beneath Thames
willows grown too obese
to resist the spate, across

Petersham Meadows, past
riverside pub and private
jetty, upstream through endless
arches of ancient crossing.

Soon I will take our daughter
so she can know the Thames,
Sweet Thames, the silent
longing and searching of Isis.

Hounslow

I
heard today
that the roof of our old house
had been ripped off by the vortex created
when the engines of a low-flying airbus made their
final approach

exposing   my first
bedroom   and its
steam   train
wall   paper

to the invisible night sky   to fly-by-wire and a testing

testing
howl
from
dark
interiors

Refugees

On arriving in NE Scotland in 1981
to teach Vietnamese Boat People

I

Early December, yet it's still autumn
in Arbroath, leaves

barely turned. Birch Path,
which the Council are offering us,

is a fine name. You can see there's good soil
in the flat land around here. There'll be work

potato picking in October,
then raspberries and strawberries in the summer.

The supermarkets are well stocked
with bamboo shoots and water chestnuts.

There's a Chinese restaurant.
We'll move here.

II

Now the Resettlement Centre
has disappeared into the dusk

and as we drive by taxi through the night
pausing at a petrol station

gulls from the nearby cliffs call
and in the distance

the blade of the Bell Rock lighthouse
cuts through a sea mist

which makes the sea look infinite
and the road ahead a road into dissolution.

Sy Mui

Sy Mui is embroidering

her eyes' point enters a wooden o
her breath swells a small stretch of cotton
to a silken bird of paradise
a silken tree of heaven
silk wings on a green silk moth

Sy Mui is embroidering

the shapes blow from her home
ripple her smile
make her fingers gently quiver

the silkworm weaves
with a slow and circular exactness
and the green moth comes to leaf

Kam-Lin and the Naturalist

He was like her, sun-beaten, but he came
from the place where he sat. A naturalist.
She was a refugee from somewhere else.

He asked her about the plants that grew there.
She said, many once.
                            'And do they still use
banana leaves to shelter from the rain?'

He smiled forward away from the cold stone,
explaining about the various species
unique to the Glen, then to rummage through
the names crushed beneath the picnic basket:
sheep's fescue, scented vernal, hairgrass, sedge—
all commoner than clover.
                            Not to her.
She picked each of the grasses he described
and made a little bunch to take her sister,
while he had discovered an orchid, fragrant,
lime-loving, yet unaccountably here
in this cold acid soil above Glen Isla.

Our Fridge

Our fridge got so iced up
that unless you shut it firmly
it'd swing back into even more ice.

When I found the yoghurts swelled,
yesterday's butter rancid
and today's milk thickening,
I blamed you,
tore the plug out in a rage
and shouting obscenities
hissed past you and into a hot bath
where I steamed all afternoon.

Now it's calm. From the kitchen
the drip of defrosting,
the return to room temperature,
a natural calming sound
like the gentle scrape of your pencil
as you sketch crimson carnations
in the sitting room.

You say you intended to shut the door.
I say I intended to defrost before.

The light goes.

The freezer's silver casket appears
above the still, cool circle of meltwater.

For Jane

As love is a word that can look plain foolish
put into verse, it's one I have avoided.
But in our thirteen years must be embedded
some words sentimentality can't polish.

How did we start? Where all affection starts:
in Mumbles, romantic cliff walks, pale sea,
strains of Sibelius, our eyes meet, agree,
and move to the satisfaction of 'hearts' . . .

No, it wasn't like that—puns and rhymes
lead the student returning home astray,
a tempting shortcut across Swansea bay,
heedless of quicksands, of high water times.

But at a bus stop: me plus fiddle-case,
you out of Zanzibar. You off to your Hall,
me back to digs. We shared lectures. That's all
that's true. A tedious coast road. Your face.

Now zoom slowly towards a lovingly made
egg custard and lines of Milton's paradise
from either side of a substantial slice
of apple crumble; then as the candles fade,

enter the cactus house in Singleton Park
and taste the orchids, let the exotic palms
sweat: do not yet hold hands, but brushing arms,
be sure to walk together home in the dark.

Three Huntingdonshire Eclogues

March, and already the winds prove it. The *Hunts Post* tells me
the mad March hare can be seen in the open field these days,
boxing or lying low; but I have yet to see one. Wind

is all I have seen, or the effects of wind: one larchlap panel
in our fence had loosened and soon the boundary line was snaking
wildly in the clay; so today a man has come with a steel rule.

The wind unnerves me. I cannot settle to anything. Instead
of putting coherent words on the page, I find my eye is drawn to
movement in the lane: green fairy wands, and winsome ragged skirts

of my neighbour's weeping willow, or my ear is hooked on the squeaky
drag of insulated cable where it coils into my study and my computer.
Then zephyrs from the window touch, like an aeolian harp, that map

of the Stonely enclosures: each strip becomes a string that sounds
an aleatory life: *Mary Hemmings Lands, Jona. Cuthberts Lands,
Geo. Rusts Lands*; there *The Orchard*, here *Great Meadow*, and where

our garden ends, the inscription *Hare Close*. The thought of a hare
concealed in that post-war enlargement, in that blank exposure,
where two dozen families scraped an anonymous living, is as chilling

as today's wind. Hares were thought to be witches' moon-creatures,
symbols of increase and of long life; seek them in stone-age caves,
Egyptian tombs; they're as elusive as fire; the hieroglyphic hare says

Exist. It suits the hare that our hedges have gone, it leaves
his ballroom free: one sunrise you may glimpse two dozen waiting
in a solemn circle; or at sunset hear one cry out like a child.

·

This morning's fierce debate (Mrs Thatcher and the Police State)
has calmed to thatched cottages and a faint aroma of pig.
Our friends, who have battered themselves all year on the tubes

and against the bars of suburban London, have come here to recover
beneath these oaks. I walk them to the Stately Home and back,
but when our neighbour's trap comes clop-clopping through the mist,

they double-glaze: a clip from a Dickens film on *Breakfast Time*.
Nor will they believe that our newsagent closes today. I explain
you cannot change things too suddenly: he had those same blinds

down when a stray bomb blew news of the war on to the cobbles.
People like their Sundays left, their pram-resistant pavement
kept as it was, along with those ghetto-blasting church-bells:

even the Co-op has to dress up in Gothic script. No, they will
never need the riot shields in Kimbolton. Cenebald knew a safe seat
when he saw one. And what would anyone want to change? Except

those few who, in scattered yet-to-be-modernised cottages (usurped
horse-kings, forgotten drovers, pleachers of hawthorn, hollers
of clay), do without double garages and swimming pools. This year two

such originals died: their names I never heard. The developers',
the builders' names, the names on the cherished number-plates—
these I can't help but know. The lanes swarm with prospective buyers

out for a spin, seeds from a tough fast-growing urban species.
Though all that ever seems to germinate is leylandii: quick-
hedging that looks like the artificial grass they drape at burials.

.

I have walked to the Warren and found there a horseshoe,
and wondered if it was truly a relic of the team-ploughing,
or just one lost by a cantering schoolgirl looking

for bridleways: and I have held it briefly like a quoit
half despising my short-lived impulse (hang it up
to catch good luck), half thrilled that I might be seeing

through its keyhole into an elm-trimmed whitethorn and
blacksmith Huntingdonshire, where our local farrier
hammered this same shoe fifty years ago, when my neighbour,

unlettered, unhurried, would have been standing watching
the sparks peal from the forge, then have followed his huge
plough horse out of the travus, over the field he had to till.

The field I cross to reach Warren Hill must have been
ten fields then: there's a machine with caterpillar treads
parked ready to eradicate these pocked strips of charred

stubble, burnt upon harvest. Respect for fire lives on—
the word in red illumination flashes as you slow down
and take the bend. Wieland is in hiding. There, where

mechanics work their deft magic on a Scandinavian combine,
and have hung one of their workshop's rusty horseshoes,
points to the earth; or in that tubular alarm calling

volunteers to out-of-control and wilful late summer
burnings: folk congregate, strangers pull over, as if
for a white wedding, and the air is specked with passion.

Roads

The first time we have let her on the road.
Her independence paid for with our fear,
as one small gold-and-silver frame goes veering
on to the verge to let a serpent-load
of scaly greens, a slurry-guzzling toad,
baleful giant, or dragon in red gear
that licks our hedges, pass. She's learnt to steer,
thank God, and signal too, the way I showed
last time we rode out. Nothing pleased her more
than my pronouncing her roadworthy, grown up
to join the brotherhood of spokeless wheels.
It's hard now to remember how it feels,
that first free-plunging run down from the top,
here on the far side of all she's waiting for.

Moving

Rooks like dust in a home
movie spatter the view
through the picture window
as we peck at belongings
in your grandmother's bungalow,
vacated now, up for sale.
The Natural History of Selborne,
an Egyptian tea towel,
rusting weights and scales . . .
What can we do with this
cracked windmill? that springless
cuckoo clock? Now that she's
bent into the storm-force
of her ninety-fifth year,
does she need this Shakespeare?

A gull outside peels like
a dressing where the barbed wire
was surgically removed
and the poppies trampled
by the intruders who came
deep in a summer's night.
Below that slope they parked
invisibly and loaded into their van
things that you do not see today.
There is no escape mechanism
ticking in the hall now.
No willow-pattern blue
to glaze the emptied rooms.
Only detritus, only utility.
Only the rooks calling for more.

Sunday, December 1998

'Life is not a stroll across a field'
  Russian proverb

A heavy frost this morning. Boots pass over the ground on wings:
the clay is defeated for a few hours. I'm out to get the paper,
escape a house full of TV and sleep, and try to accept
my father's death. Through the hawthorn hedge that today I will
cut to half its height, pleaching, layering, remembering how useless
I am at any other gardening jobs, how my father rejoiced in every
patch he had ever worked, from Kew to Hounslow, from Eastcote to the Peaks.
There's little traffic. No birds. A moon stoops above those wretched
cowering trees that still survive: a middle English landscape
stripped and made to bear the worst for half a century, the farmers'
experimental camp for the extermination of species, the breeding of a heroic
    grain—
what happens (the Ministry enquires) if you uproot all the hedges, let the oaks
choke in mid-field, trail fertiliser dregs along the ditches,
plough right through the quick of the land, and spray spray spray?

Each day my father endured his two injections, a diabetic
forty years; each day he'd devour a thick book
of medicaments, for heart, for blood, for eyes, for toes; each day
a battle with what time makes of chronic illness, turning the sweetness
of spring mornings to sour November moods, which was when he died,
before I had had time to call. Weeks since I walked here: the Kym a congealed
fiddling, while the Goyt goes on pumping its grand opera below
his empty seat. To look down on that flow from the Marple flight
of sixteen locks through almost sixteen years, or to enter the haunt
of kingfishers he could never see, surviving instead so many decades
in the waste land of his illness, an existence as glacial and elf-riddled
as the Iceland where his youth first erupted: called up to the crust
of a passionate inner warmth, the war, those friends, that missing diary,
Morse runes from a distant unknown territory, translated and passed on . . .

This is the sluice, the little pool I always said I would bring
Dad to see, but never did. There is quite an outpouring
in spite of the logjam, memorial elm and alder, spent shells
of birch, pontoons of sycamore ash elder, froth and waste.

The morning's frost, the clear sky, the sun, have tuned the scene
to a Christmas carol note of purity. The footpath ends at the butcher's,
low moaning from the slaughterhouse. How many in their stripes
have earned a living from dead meat here since the First War?
And I beyond that high wall since the Falklands, playing with words.
An urn of sterile ash, a cold calm pallor on the slab
of softness where my mother sits weeping, reaching out, waiting for
change, for answers, the unshrouding and silent rise of a heron
from the river bed, where it could not possibly have been hiding,
to glide, untroubled in its grey authority, out of this morning.

The Statute Fair

The caravans begin to gather on the green outside Kimbolton
weeks before the date. The Statute fair has come
round again, and our medieval village honours its eighth

century of trade—in men, in stock, and now in leisure.
St. Audrey watches from the Fens as her one gift to the language
is unvoiced from every noisy pitch, each loser's

prize (for every child must win today) doled out
by wretched souls who show not a glimmer of that fun they hurl
as hatred at the world. Take your inflatable hammer, or your stuffed

blue whale. The Statty Fair. Its hate-beat can be heard
across the parish. Its tawdry colours spout out of tradition's
trench like Very lights. We cannot hear ourselves

but fix a grin and load a stick with sugar spinning
like our sweet spun brains within our skulls, watching
those kids up on the waltzer. Adam in his gatehouse grimaces

but Vanbrugh knows this is the Restoration spirit.
Forget what passed within these houses during the Commonwealth.
Forget the witch-hunts and the families divided: bite your toffee-apple,

buy your token for the dodgems, and bump your brother, bump
your neighbour, but don't ask their religion, or whether they believe
in monarchs, or if the shops in Huntingdon should open on Sunday.

from Huntingdonshire Nocturnes

Fairey

The first public conjuring show I gave
    in the wake of my small ad—
        'YOUNG AMATEUR MAGICIAN . . .'—was at
Fairey Aviation. I can't believe

I barnstormed (what was I then, thirteen?)
    the swell of a hundred faces,
    unveiling chrome surprises
to a tongue roll, pulling out of spin

and sleight and patter, wand-tip
    abracadabras, and a trail
    of paper-flower applause. Unreal
as an adolescent dream you wake from, grown up

and disbelieving. Can that really have been me
    piloting that vintage Fairey
    whose one prestigious aerial
manoeuvre was to turn and dive for the sea?

Magic

The loss of magic, where did it go, is what
spellbinds me. I was made to look at it,
was invited to touch it, thrust my hand
through it, inspect it briefly from all sides.
It was more real than any mirror-gazing
church service. It pupated from the deaths
of those whose houses were the fairy dells
of the pantomimes they took us to, ogres
transformed to mice, old men to dames, and girls—
all flesh a made-up wonder! It involved
Christmas and countryside and seven planets.
It was hidden in the shellac oyster beds
of school assembly, or in the dog's horn.
When I dug a hole between huge peonies,
through layers of Thames alluvium and clay
I was searching for its source. When I wrote
a story set in the remotest corner
of Chobham Common, I was summoning it.
My father used to do a trick with money:
a coin that vanished would appear wrapped up
inside a nest of boxes. Although I knew
it did not grow on trees—how slow to ripen,
that black-and-white TV!—this was a power
and it could be learnt. An Easter conjuror
performed at primary school, and even when
his Cinderella left a few of her rags,
my friends all jeering in disgust, I saw
prestige in the role. Perhaps this was just
to do with puberty: the thrill of pleasure
in 'Colour Change Cords' an escape rope down
from adult searchlights; the 'Vanishing Lady'
a passage to force through beneath high voltage
to the erotic free world. It was not
what I wanted, though I let my future hang
behind its lavish silk, show-stopping, chrome.
Sesame! and my childhood's gone, but magic
beyond the David Nixon show, beyond

From the Word-house

for Stuart Henson

It would decay, the Word-house, books and all
these drafts and notebooks, LPs, CDs, hard drive
or software, if I didn't try to give
the boards a yearly coat of Cuprinol
to keep the weather off. No inch of wall,
yet this foxed sheet has managed to survive
my every clear-out—lines that somehow live
beyond their frame, in which you draw the well

outside my study, make of it a source,
a future 'way back down', as you here coin it
in free verse, fresh, unmoulded, from your Brickyard.
For home is where we most explore, of course,
when struggling through a thank-you note or sonnet.
It finds us, like an unexpected postcard.

Quotidian

A life held together by little rituals: choosing
foam or gel; wetting the razor, and wondering whose
bleary face this is in the small round glass.

Preparing the cafetiere with two portions decaf
to one of the real thing, anticipating the safe
landing of toast on plate. Spread the Flora. Enough

jam to keep the diet quiet. Turf the cat
from your chair as you do your balancing act to where you've sat
for thirty years to have this breakfast. No chat,

as that would be uncivilised, though returning
from her morning walk, Jane tells me it's raining.
Radio 4. I try to mute the Business, burning

my mouth with coffee, spilling it (and jam) on the Sports
page as the cat prepares to jump up. Now, Thought
for the Day: my bloody blood pressure tablets. Abort.

from Huntingdonshire Codices

Sweet Chestnut

Maturity is to know the star-shakes
in your heart. It is to have turned aside

and, despite the upright and the smooth, gone on
turning. It is to be twisting free of

one's roots, ascending to its very lip
the twin helix. To have observed each year

some fresh disfiguring lump. To have felt
the next ring splitting under the renewed weight

of spring. It is to have seen the spears
lifted, then a spiked mace.

On slopes of ash to have faced the eruption
of your griefs. To have flowered. To propagate.

Three Huntingdonshire Elegies

Stonely is a still life as August approaches: the hanging
begonias glow amber and red on the edge of decay.
The cat ignores a manic thrush at her nose, under swinging

strands of crumbling Himalayan Musk. Already the birds
have vowed they'll leave music to the wasps, to breezes
in the ash tree's first dry minor keys, and to half-heard

falsettos out of Luton, into Stansted. There is a ticking in the hedge.
That vacuum you took apart: its canary yellow filter
rocks on the patio. Was there talk of ordering an oven, a fridge

before the offers close? Nobody moves from their green chairs.

.

Fog, the first of the season, blurs our garden's parallels
and frost graces the lawn, the rotary drier's web,
the plants that no one has dead-headed, old mountain-bike wheels.

The weeping cherry planted for our silver wedding (and severed
straight after in a single act of negligence) is beginning
to reassert its habit over the tumbled green chairs of summer.

There is a glaze across the pond and our one fish, veteran
of the heron wars, is a hologram reminder of lost gold.
Ash keys hang unrattled; shrivelled hips and deep-veined

ivy hide the remains of an elder. The ladder is still
against the shed where we keep all that the children have outgrown,
where adolescence has mildewed magic, animal, doll

and picture book, where Christmases fade. The birch and apple
are like Gabriel and one of Scrooge's ghosts. There is a hosannah
and some humbug in the hedge as next-in-line saplings

wake from a recurring dream of being spears, of resisting
the villa and—that field our donkey brayed in twenty years—
the grove and lake and jetty, newly cut and pasted,

smiling in soft focus. Out of the gloom, a developer
fiddling on the roof, considers the best way of blocking
natural light, of draining time through plastic and fibre,

of keeping history out. But the climate has got there first,
with its impressionist demands. You can almost hear Monet
talking, driving a hard bargain and sealing it with mist.

.

The mother at the end of Hatchet Lane howls for her calf.
The field at the back of our house—all spiky set-aside—drains
away the incessant January rains. There is sunshine enough

to make these walkers believe it's spring. The squirrels are already
converts and they hurry to worship. Over the barbed wire
where sludge from the lake was spread, there's movement. Sunday

is creeping to life and I am holding a carbon festival of wreath
and bough, shrub sacrifice, fence and trellis offerings.
Fire blazes and I hose it down. As I prod, from beneath

the griddled sticks—a hedgehog, writhing, horribly scorched.
What should I do? Try drowning it in the pond? No use,
it swims, so I hook it on the fork, dump it under the hedge

and wait for the fire to burn down. My conscience hibernates,
while—out of the embers—nails, staples, screws raise their
accusing prickles at me. The creature vanishes overnight.

Cataclysm

Higher, louder, the hum.
A pair of stars colliding.
It's in the newspaper,

but this is coming from
our Fred, who's seen a rival
in the forsythia. Circling,

the neutered one made gold
by the morning sun, the black
and platinum, still closer,

spiralling inwards, until
violently they merge to a ripple
through space-time that surges

the length of our back garden
only to collapse as I call him
into a hole in the hedge.

17th October 2017

Compleat

To set off on my bike at first light,
pass through the gates and down the avenue
of horse chestnuts towards Robert Adam's
creation, the low roar of the M4 ahead,
and of the Great West Road

and take from its light brown nylon sleeve
the varnished split-cane lengths of my rod
and fit them together, attach the multiplying
reel with its fine line of a breaking strain
I can't now recall,

fasten the hook, using a knot, however,
I can remember (around three times
and back through the loop), adding the float,
a simple quill like the kind of pen Dickens
or even Shakespeare used,

scattering groundbait, before kneeling
to open a tin of maggots like the contents
of a skull, its imagery, stick one on the barbed
point of the hook, or pierce the flesh of a lugworm
dug from a sea mist,

so to cast, to feel the free line
sizzle across the surface and its speed ravel
off the unclamped reel: then to sit
on the edge of the lake at Osterley Park
quite lost in watching,

was a joy, an intensity of youthful delight
no poet could capture, though I only ever
caught roach, some minnows, not the long desired
bottom-feeding tench, nor the tremendous
episcopal rainbow.

English

Awre

It is a hopeful name to be born to.
It promises Spring; it sings of pickings
from a lost family orchard, an Eden

on Severn banks, a fruit that is ripe
yet always green. Hold it to your cheek
for the faint enigma. Lick it, your tongue

buds an estuary. Cast, it will bob
the equinox deep into English
etymologies: grig and girn and groin . . .

Watch it running on a playing field
with others of the inner city, picked on,
nicknamed, yellowed to a cartoon brat.

Or beneath the hundred thousand crosses
left by men who could never spell
themselves, imagine it grinning from their skulls

or groaning in the pelvic bones of women
who bore it, a surge from this serpent bend
of the river into every green corner.

Awre on the River Severn is one of the places where the name Greening was first noted. On one of the few occasions I included the poem in a reading, there happened to be someone from the tiny village in the audience, who told me that Greenings had only just returned to live there. I was, dare I say it, Awre-struck. JG

The Oak

Approaching the perimeter, the boy
who dreams of *Down the Bright Stream*, and the man
who knows *Guernica*. The boy who will ask
what oak apples are, and the man who won't
explain that they are tumours. The boy who hopes
to spot a red squirrel. The man who says
they will all prove grey.
                  My childhood and I
may never have danced Hey Derry Down as
our forefathers danced around the oak, but
we have learnt to read the signs that tell us
THESE WOODS ARE PRIVATE.
                      Thick arteries
have thickened until they shiver behind
this ragged blanket. Young companies
of hazel that wriggle their golden tassels
in a lithe floorshow fascinate and stir
the man. The boy looks up at a jigsaw sky.

A Wicked Witch, The Thunderer, or a Phantom?
The words on the wire repeat their one sound.
These woods, These woods—like a stock dove begging—
These woods have danced a navy on their knees,
are War Office Property and have been
since the Ice Age, since the first battering rams.
Five hundred varieties of riddle
and song: the woodpecker attack, plain cuckoo,
or a brace of cruise. These woods are private,
and since we can read, we shall not trespass.

But words have not yet heard of literacy.
Outlaws, half wild, they will flee with Rimbaud
to the forest, hide there, seem to have helped
manoeuvre your woolly thoughts into a pen—

but then leap out at you, tear at your heart.
They'll not come to your knife, but screech and squeal
like sawmills to be fed.
                    Robin Hood's Larder.
The Royal Oak. The Parliament Oak.
The Oak of William the Conqueror, and
Harry's Oak. Oaks that were pulpits.
Oaks that were gibbets. Oaks that are jokes and
resemble naked men. The oak that Hitler
gave to a public school. The haunted oaks.
The stranded oaks. The oak of the artist
or poet. The commemorative oaks.
And oaks strapped round for forty feet of circumference
that simply sprang up wild from a roadside hedge.
The oak that was an acorn on an oak
that grew as Christ grew.
                         These words are public
and this side of the perimeter fence.
There have been songs to which no creature knows
the words and words which nothing—not the raven
on Odin's shoulder, not the writing desk
veneered like the chart of a distant sound—
can solve.
            Pieces indistinguishably blue.

Gathered where they dropped but cannot germinate,
brought to the open, free of history,
free of the long shadow, they may be saved
from extinction, which is in every cup.

The London Plane

A frost rang early with the results:
cling, now, to your life's short year, for each
of its yellowing days must let the five senses

twist, then drop, until you are naked asleep.
Awake—patched, yet with hardly a wrinkle—
you stretch and bend to shade the truth from us,

but must submit, an ashen almost-skeleton,
to be avenued in soot-free, showerless white,
falling in with these others, octogenarians also—

survivors of the repeated spring raids,
hawkers of a century's detritus, Londoners—
Londoners to your lacewood core.

Allow, gradually, the soft expansion from beneath
that rigid bark to shuck whatever poverty
or close-grained prejudice could not resist.

Hug your next year's buds. Accept
and protect the swelling in the hollow stem
of each hour, each last breath, until the day falls.

Birch

Canoe or witch's
broom at the bottom

of the garden: escape
from the day of fire

or the day the scalp-
chilling icecaps

grind their warpath
and our only comfort

against the red clay
in which we bury

frozen hoards
of gold and silver

is gold and silver
of the forest malls

where we will live on
postcards, bootsoles,

pennybuns and
bark-bread, bark-bread.

The English Dream

The English dream of nothing as grimy
as a coal mine, but of a filigree past,
nothing as real as a steel industry—
they would prefer to do without the last
two hundred years and live in a century
they imagine to have been, where good taste
was a knot garden, not a chip factory.
Revolutions can change too much too fast . . .
so we sit, and we soak up glossy brochures
touching the gilded realms of William Morris,
in easy chairs hand-wrought from English oak,
leafing through woods and streams and air as pure
as celluloid, where shepherds woo Chloris
with ingenious rhymes, and there's no work.

The Apprentice House, Styal

And did those feet
clatter down the cobbles
to the mill for thirteen hours
each day, and at night—
through stitchings of torn light—
stamp to keep out the cold,
then cram into shared boxes?

Not so long ago . . .
Your grandmother's mother could tell
what crossed the young girls' eyes
into their escape routes, what came
nibbling from the attic where the oats
for the day's cold porridge
were stored alongside corpses.

Of those who forgot
to raise their hands in gratitude,
to lower their heads in time
when crawling under the black
shuddering looms of (charity,
child labour, brimstone
and treacle) their new Jerusalem.

Rollright

What draws so many people from TV
on a dull Sunday to walk in this slow
circle around the Rollright Stones? Could it be

dissatisfaction with December's video
gloss, the Christmas fast-forward family
rushes? Our bright, bitter Hollywood show?

To be, for a moment, a grey ungainly
buffalo, slow-treading the sakiyeh wheel
through a life on the banks of prehistory,

sustaining a narrow strip of a real
fecundity, inch-thick, and holding off
the desert that rips on either side. To feel

briefly a familiar, gritty and bluff
scrubbing of the back of our century
by something pocked like pumice, patchy-rough—

truth that our well-adjusted eyes can't see
but pangs deep back in the mouth when we breathe
how here we sense an electricity

that still survives after such weathering,
such decay . . . ? Or is it merely a way
of switching from one channel to another,

after which we slope back to our cars to lay
hands on our sacred plastic circles, hold
the silver keys of our life out, and pray

through fumes of exhaust, for something less old.

Causeway

Imagine all those dark
timbers revealed
in the damp, dripping
square of Flag Fen:

the sinister causeway
a family tree
that endures beneath
our flat screen lives,

our futile speed-
dating fertility
quest, a huddle
of lost responsibilities.

We look back through
the surface they believed
was the way in
to a better world—

the sacrifices, broken
implements, battlefield
trophies, the lines
of splintered promises,

invisible and unable to
survive once exposed.
Slowly eaten by sugars,
they will dry out

and die under the glare
of children powered by
a new electricity
generated where the

causeway is pointed
that charges their phones,
their games, their pods
as they drop into the darkness.

Richard III

That King Richard was a child murderer,
This every child knows.

                                    Out on the moors
I first learned not to absorb bitterness
or let it perish the soul. I was seven,
had seen my uncle and my brother killed,
my father's head impaled on Micklegate Bar.

That King Richard was a child murderer . . .

I learned to deflect my darker instincts
off a bleak smile, to make a sole companion
of the moor. Once, let a Jervaulx monk expound
my sinfulness; later, a veteran
of Agincourt teach me to ride and use
the longbow.   That King Richard was a child—
King Richard the Third . . .

                                        When I was thirteen,
I was brought to watch the Woodvilles dancing
my brother, King Edward, to their golden tunes
on the terraces of Greenwich and of Shene.
I suffered their jeers, smiled, but did not see
in their dance how they were already weaving
from the red briar and the white a garth
to trap the truth.

                            That King Richard the Third,
O Tudors . . .
                    That the pure reputation
I carried south from Wensleydale to share
was to be adulterated with a butt
of Malmsey, and two small velvet bundles.

Fotheringhay

Fragments of what England
used to be, tucked
in corners of September:

a park, with its oaks
like a dining room in
a stately home, thrown

open to the public, but
cordoned to keep the sheep
and their deep-pile

instincts, their appetites,
their Sunday cries of
ah! and *ah!* from coming

to the table. Turf
reseeded, so we may
browse where we belong.

    .

Who keeps doves now? In
Eaglethorpe—where a girl,
out jogging, flusters

past me into the woods—is
a perfect dovecote. Not
just for good luck, but

to feed the golden manners
of the Lord in his great eyrie;
squabs, white as her breath-

lessness, feel the knife
pierce them to the board,
know his hidden talons.

    .

Sheep rise, and there is a
ripple across the sky, as if
the master of its domain

with his four-wheel drive
had printed a snakeback
cirrus track, and then appeared,

making his broadcast, hands
in a nitrates bag, redeployed,
bright yellow, full of the day.

.

Past preaching doves, towards
a steady tolling bell,
calling the congregations

that are gone. A water
meadow comes to feel
precious on such a morning.

A man could be a divining Y
held by the earth, and I
a jaywalker between spires.

.

The way is not direct
to that eight-sided crown,
but through a web, a zig-

zag of scaffolded planking
across the dry ducts of
a floodplain that knows only

guttural until February.
A sluice gate hangs like
a guillotine. Poplars press

to watch the matronym on a
pleasure craft descend into
the cold print of a lock.

.

The weir race holds forth
through all mere prattling
and there is no barrier

to stop a child falling.
No Fishing, the sign says,
but the footpath casts

towards brown eddies where
these meadows end and the church
vane is a spinning lure.

.

A lantern tower to guide
huntsmen home through
Rockingham Forest, which no

visitor finds, except in
his mind, meandering
between bare fields towards

where the boar first
charged, and the red
deer lay down her false

antlers. A man in shirt-
sleeves, a camera slung
around him, leaps a stile.

The light is perfect for
a photograph of the
castle that is not there.

.

Soliloquise—don't
hurry along this green
lane, there is too much

history to be plotted.
This does not feel like
paths you have walked

on other Sundays, nor is it
because you are escaping
tensions at home, your new-

born nephew in the house,
his birthday forever
September; no, it is

the enormity of this small
hamlet you have so long
procrastinated in reaching.

·

How our own expectations
surprise us: the mound
where I had imagined

I would imagine Mary
Queen of Scots' last
toss of the head and

thread of Latin, Richard
the Third's first loss and
Yorkish howl, is today

common ground, a flag
with 'Caravan Club'
jauntily planted on the site

of the block, and a tartaned
weekender boorishly
munching bacon in the sun.

·

Overlooking a smell of
black plasticky hay
and molasses, in a loop

of the Nene, the motte
seethes like a forgotten
corpse. September's end,

and hotter than it should be,
as if the world were just
beginning to sweat at

some of the past wrongs
only now it's old enough
to feel and regret.

   .

Twin toddlers slide
down the path from
the keep; a man

and a woman restrain
an Alsatian. I inspect
two plaques on a fence

interning one fragment
of a refuge. The river
curves irretrievably.

   .

Nowhere to sit without
getting pricked or stung
to watch a power-

cruiser pass, or listen
to that robin try
to voice past freezings.

   .

No day is adequate,
no life, to take in
what this hand's-breadth

offers up: but only to sit
like a stylite on one
high moment, is as much

profundity as a Sunday
in a working week
will allow, or the rev-

rev of a congregation
reversing past holes
in the sky, or the boring

pneumatic noises
people make—civil
teachers and engineers.

.

The church has a sign
on the door warning me
no valuables are inside.

Instead, everything is
out for harvest: a glazed
plait on the altar, pears,

pumpkins, marrows, eggs,
love-apples great and small;
along with the jars of

yellow pickly heat and rape-
flower honey . . . No valuables.
All is empty, secure.

.

Fotheringhay brings
home to me these natural
thoughts from the richest

soils of England. One
native pine and a hump
of briar are the last

flickerings of sleeping
booty; now autumn is
no longer rusty witchlocks,

but sun kisses earth from
open skies where hair
rises a manchet white.

                    .

The plea a village pond
makes when it's frozen
and a beer can strikes,

the sound of everyday
returning, the freezing
over of whatever warm

song came streaming today:
those trusty paratroopers
up in the trees palisading

the church—the rooks—pick
at Midland clay as if they
hoped to resurrect a forest.

                    .

A parachutist has been
released from a small
private cross, to become

micropolyphony: a whelk,
a periwinkle, in the blue
Sunday tides; it drifts

his/her hazy way down
with another and now
others like seeds from some

vanished theme, which yet soars
over the church, a falcon
freed of its fetterlock.

White Cliffs

Whistling round into Shakespeare Cliff, where poor
Mad Tom led his blind father to the verge
of devotion, my only daughter saw
from the carriage window the darkness surge
in upon her. I comfort her with talk
appropriate to her three months of light,
sweet nothings such as Lear perhaps once spoke
to his beloved fool, before the night
tunnelled his wits. Still she will not settle.
I would have tried to lull her with that long
blank verse speech of Edgar's if I thought beetle,
chough or crow talked peace. But she wants a song,
so *There'll be bluebirds over . . .* Searchlights sweep
above these black white cliffs, and she's asleep.

For the Six Wives

My brother's wife, but only I loved Catherine:
no woman did I ever trouble more
to be the mother of my kingdom's heir,
to consummate my first, my last, desire.
She failed, and still I travel to her, farther
than dreams can ride, into her castle blackness.

While black-eyed, six-fingered Anne, all blackness—
but yellow for the funeral—round Catherine
danced, and so miscarried, leaving me father
to no son, but to the death of More and more.
The French blade of a sonneteer's desire
took off the goggle-eyed brunette, which done, ere

I had half composed a twisting hybrid air
and walked the paths of polyphonic blackness,
I found in fresh green leaves my heart's desire.
Since neither the Marquess Anna, nor Catherine
of Aragon would give, let plain Jane Seymour
be the mother, and I at last the father

to the name of his father's mother's father,
King Edward. Fog clears, sun explodes the air.
Queen Jane lies back exposed on Childbed Moor
bleeding into her last puerperal blackness.
And I must seek a wife, another Catherine,
an Anne. But all I find when I desire

are dreams that buck, a face that cleaves desire,
a Flanders nightmare come to lure me farther
from my senses. Until a fifth, a Catherine
comes pumping down my dropsied, ulcered skin, air
off Venus' mount, bubbling eruptive blackness:
I rise! I sing!—for a breve. For hundreds more

lie in Mistress Catherine's score. And the maw
of Traitor's gate gapes wide. Some say desire
for heads is for maidenheads, that the blackness

gathered in these my good looks proves them father
to impotence, one nine-year-old their heir.
But winch me here, and I will show them, Catherine . . .

(And you, Catherine, that if you had given more—
bequeathed me one male heir—this one desire
had flamed no farther, the rest had been sweet blackness.)

At Steeple Gidding

As he leans on his
white van, I notice
the tell-tale device.

Found anything? —*Well . . .*
He gives a faint smile,
and takes out a small

square box to remove
the broken silver
disc inside, half a

penny someone lost
when Edward the First
was king, and forest

reigned instead of field,
and they'd yet to build
this church in the wild.

A door into the
fourteenth century
swings open as he

lowers that rare coin
on to my palm, then
closes once it's gone

as if to tell us
nothing of value's
left in God's old house.

Crossing the Heath

to Penelope Shuttle

Twenty-four thousand times in any year, lightning strikes
and kills. On the Heath, the timber shells, like bony Flemish spires,
point heavenwards in warning. The stags take note and bow their heads
at the sky's first challenge, or hurl a bellowing peal back in defiance.

Quicken your pace. Ask for Belfont, Bedfound, Bedefunde, Beda's spring,
however the changes ring, where he dispatched his woman each morning
from their heap of halfsmart, crosswort, bloodcup, from under their thatch,
to fetch even in such storms, even when she had reached nine months . . .

When will it end, this barrenness, these waves of agony, barefoot
through lynchet, dyke, furze, thistle, the gusts and groans, water
breaking overhead? Beda's woman lies back in the heather bed
of history; you press on. At your feet is a baby, and another,

heads like mushrooms, crowning, crying, put out for the Heath
to take care of. Their mewings pierce the air. But there is no milk.
Do not pick them. Leave them to the *dama dama* who gather round.
Consider instead the oaks, each ring another year that these

might have suffered. Pass on through Hag's Lane into Bedfont. *Spring
with a drinking vessel.* Old English *byden*, a tub or container,
funta, on loan from Rome (whose roots and tesserae lie scattered
beneath your modern tread), *fons* or *fontus.* That distant rumbling

is just a farmer bringing home grain. They are far behind you now
between dead oaks and dark enclosing deer, exposed, yet silent.
Thunder has paused. Head for the church, the fighting cocks (or peacocks)
of St Mary the Virgin, East Bedfont, and hurry on through its topiary

nonsense, past the tombs of those who died on February the 31st,
or aged three hundred and sixty-one. Enter the pudding-stone.
At the font like a cowled servant presenting the first and final course,
is a Friar, sworn to poverty, chastity, his vessel raised, fending off storms.

Uffington

Secretions of a primitive
vision no one can see
except from a plane:

a plain whispering
horse words beneath
its high-yield wheat.

We tell our children
mysteries in chalk.
Do they think it's cool?

It's school, and it's cold.
They want the car,
not a horse's eye.

I watch the vapour trail's
airy lore erased
from a white board,

bored children turning
away. But I still don't
know enough—

Uffington only answers
to the sky and never
teaches earth why

white horses were
corralled here
by history, her secret.

Sulis Minerva in Stonely

You would not know there was an ancient well
behind this forsythia, until it rains
and then you hear that hollow passing bell
tolling a pure life laid down for the mains,

reminding you of rabbits loosely slung
within its cool, damp lip by the gamekeeper,
of that old woman someone told you flung
herself into its gullet. The well is deeper

than common sense might think: down sixteen feet,
past snail and weed and slime, the plumb-bob rests
on things you cannot know. The only date
it utters is a zero, the only guests

it sings of are those who in passing fed
a coin, a bell, a jewel down its throat
or—earlier still—a skull, a severed head.
Its one response, that grateful bottom note.

To Pepys, near Huntingdon

I almost think I'll pass you on your way
out from your uncle's house. In the Country Park.
At Brampton Garden Centre. On this bike-
and jogging-path, your wig framed by the grey
remains of gravel pits. Between the A-
roads' tightly fastening knot. Down that dry track
behind the church, perhaps, since it would take
you to the Bull Inn. Or—most likely place—
at Hinchingbrooke, your ghost still making merry
with the Montagus. Removed from any thought
of holding out with pen and coded diary
against fire, plague, brothel, commonwealth, court;
but watching milkmaids slink from Portholme dairy,
while somewhere a standard's raised, a war is fought.

George III at Kew

You think me mad, but I have just returned
from a landscape new beyond anything
imaginable at Kew. It seemed I passed
through the perimeter wall and out away
from all formality, a blur of years,
a riffle of trees, to where a figure stood
in skins. He told me what man needed was
a burrow, that these baubles could be swept
out of the window, that nothing is nobler
than digging in the dirt. He pointed to
my straitjacket and called it what our age
deserved, then turned to where his hatchet stood
and started to hew an oak. I looked in vain
for my old pleasure-grounds, for any walks
or prospects—no lake, but just a pond, without
form or ornament. What a place, I thought,
for Capability . . . But now this fellow
had raised his axe to make the final cut:
'All this you lost.' At which my senses cleared,
I woke here at the Temple of Victory,
and knew exactly where I had been transported.

Greenway House

for J

Every night you read yourself to sleep
with an Agatha Christie—
the broken spines and ghastly covers
hang over our bed, the green head
with its bulging eye, the pestle
and mortar, some tablets, a rope.
It's an odd kind of lullaby.

But now your dream has brought us
to Greenway itself, where the paths
climb and intertwine like fugal
plot arrangements (the Boat House,
the Battery) above the estuary
as it darts a half-glimpsed
solution through distracting trees.

And you can sleep easy, *Dead
Man's Folly* slipping from
your fingers, the ferry sailing
across to the other side where
they know all the answers,
the victims laid out for inspection,
everyone gathered in the library.

Satellite

A dish points outwards from our outside wall
to what we cannot see: stars that know all
more clearly than these nightly Movie Greats
the fate of earthen empires. The new estates
that blinker us from crystal ballroom spaces,
haul us on in their fibre-optic traces,
plough constellations; with a flash of shares
u-turning, leave the Great and Little Bears
extinct and gilt-edged bars of progress furrowed
down the land's face. All that we have is borrowed:
museums full of stuffed trophies slowly
decaying. Territories that tick. Holy
marbles seeming to breathe. Even these words I
mix to purity, and this island time
we live on, living off serials, then soap,
and lastly just news—that shooting green hope
our parents plotted as the world turned red,
not with sunset, nor shame, but foreign dead.
We wait, hungry, now we have cleaned the Great
from Britain, scraped it out, shrunk it, wait
for a force beyond this uttermost storey
of our high rise, a column whose glory
will be to have relieved us of our fame,
of all that mafficking, cheering of a name
picked blind from a skull and nailed to the sky.
The dish receives its message from on high
in beams that swaddle the earth, in curves
of parabolic reckoning, then serves
us word made flesh: chained bare Salome sprawled
before us, while Civilisation's bald
chronicler slots between those repeats of Wars
for King and Country networked in the stars.

Flight

Heath Row

A jet tips tail first towards the runway
where the tarmac has started to gleam and steam
and peel itself back revealing hardcore, then gravel,

then loam, then clay, a flint-flicker of glass
passing, flowers into bulbs, beanstalks to shoots,
sails slowing to ungrind wheat from manchet,

to heath that is bog that is scrub that is forest
clearing, clearing so a sarsen can now rise
for this reverse procession of darkening beards

where blood is uncongealed into a newly membered
body, led below deramifying mistletoe
on oak trees that have begun to shrink to nothing

but thunder followed by lightning and an up-pour to the
horizon of ice fronts, advancing, retreating
as the earth shudders, floods, howls, ignites.

Lessons

The plane carrying Geography passes over towards Heathrow
　　and it says *The map I am following is signed Speed*

The plane carrying History passes over towards Heathrow
　　and it says *Here is the paper. I have folded it into a dart.*

The plane carrying Chemistry passes over towards Heathrow
　　and it says *My cauldron! My crucible! My melting pot!*

The plane carrying Physics passes over towards Heathrow
　　and it says *Boom!* but only after it has vanished

The plane carrying Biology passes over towards Heathrow
　　and it says *Fly Pandemic. Jet Lag. DVT.*

The plane carrying Maths passes over towards Heathrow
　　and it says *Given that you have real roots, go figure*

The plane carrying Art passes over towards Heathrow
　　and it says as it brushes Green Belt with its shadow

'The plane carrying Design passes over towards Heathrow
　　and has a better idea'

The plane carrying Religious Studies passes over towards
　　Heathrow (spire, minaret) looking for crop circles

The plane carrying French, Spanish, German, Chinese, Gujarati,
　　passes over towards Heathrow and says nothing

The plane carrying English passes over towards Heathrow
　　and keeps on going

To Icarus

Have confidence. It can be done, because
I know. This is not poetry, but science.
These wings are real. Just feel them. Try them on.
Have confidence in me. You know all flight
is binary, a balance held between
the earth's pull and the air. Like father, like son.
Those birds you helped dissect, do you recall
the counterpoint of their flight feathers? Learn
to use these wings as they do when they sing.
This is plain thread, left over from a reel
unwound within my labyrinth. And that
is wax. Have confidence in your own limbs.
Our aim is to overcome the one last
barrier, to ascend as high as I
have tunnelled deep, to find that other centre
Minos failed to reach (who could not recognise
his soul's tyrannic roar): the speck, the egg,
the tiny lark-like trill of liberty.
My only fear is of your fearfulness.
You never rushed to be the first one down
a slide, to swing across the void, to plumb
deep waters. Son, the truth is we are too close.
Believe you can do more than I have taught.
Aim high. Be light-hearted. Listen to me.

Summer Wings

I feed the fish, wondering how long now this old pond liner can be expected to last,
and as the gold moons rise, crater-mouthed, to meet my cosmic shower
a pair of wings brushes me. Looking up, the snow-peaked blue
has become a nursery slope for swallows—such sheer joy
in their slalom, even this grey wood pigeon (piston
to their supersonic) tries a few manoeuvres,
comically clapping his own ungainly
hedge-hop. Everything wants
to fly, from fish rising

on their swim bladders
to dragonflies who hoard the sun
jewelled surface to flame at tortoiseshell
and peacock on their quest for the buddleia grail,
to starling-chat, dove-coo, chaffinch-prattle, wren-click
of the buried fibre-optic tree lines August has not yet silenced.
Soon, too, there will be owls and a bat, but first the approaching whine
of a microlight, three spitfires from Old Warden, a balloon procession sighing
for vanished meadow, or, once it is night, the swift, clear cursor of a passing satellite.

Homecoming—To My Family

Hölderlin: 'Heimkunft—An die Verwandten'

I

Out on the Heath, night still glows as approaching images
   shine in the pleasure of travel and skim the pre-war semis.
From Staines to Bell Corner, screeching broomsticks blast
   above rowan, birch and maidenhair with a sly wink.
Slowly the rush hour struggles around its eagerness to get away—
   children or hardened travellers, all squabbling affectionately
between hotel and multistorey: it accelerates, brakes,
   speeds off again to the drunkenness of imminent escape.
There, a year is nothing but endless holidays, a shuffling
   sleight of lands on the pilgrim arrivals and departures board.
The Bird of Thunder, meanwhile, stacked high and circling,
   knows all destinations and announces that day is about to break.
Below, curtains are pulled back on bedroom windows
   and from duvets each cold eye meets this high processional.
They know expansion is inevitable; they have heard the groaning by night
   (as others before heard druids), the reversing engines howl,
spilling kerosene, ruining maths lessons, music recitals.
   The engineers never cease, night or day. It is a gift.

II

Peacefully glittering, the silver tubes pass over
   the clouds, rose-tinted above their Himalayan snowline,
and higher still beyond the stratosphere, the unblinking orbits
   of the future trace their plans, the shuttles, stations, satellites
and whatever unspoken possibilities the *deus ex machina* decides
   as it looks down clairvoyant on the cloud the age has created
for its pleasure, for its pastimes: enough wire to entangle ourselves
   but not to hang with these highwaymen at the Bell where new developments—
the mall and leisure centre and luxury apartments—proclaim
   green shoots for the drought-afflicted, an ozone summer,
the cumulus humilis drifting, the windsock proud.
   Even that slow cortege towards the crematorium seems
off on the journey of a lifetime as, passing the demolished Regal,

you recall *The Sound of Music* or where Memorydiscs began
your first *Unfinished* and something touches the very depths, opening
　　choice and opportunity, trams changing to trolleybuses
then Green Lines and now an express out to the departures lounge
　　on the Heath and a joyful urge to fly off to pastures new.

III

Addressing the unknown—that's always been the business of poetry,
　　so I've done my stretch with religion, with angels, spirits and the rest,
hoping for the best. Who hasn't drawn alongside a prayer
　　watching the news, thinking what if that refugee in Afghanistan
or Iraq were me—and thinking too of the Boat People
　　we set out to help, their thanks, their constant smiling, while our own
parents had pulled an empire down about their ears, pirates
　　drowning in powerlessness? Meantime, I am rocked by the bus,
raised from wheelchair level, the driver jokes about the weather
　　and laughs (*taken our bus lanes, innit*) at Olympians, as he cruises
through the shadow of my grammar school, through tenses, cases, subjects,
　　veils and hoods and tattoos, rolling me up to the bus stop.
It's warm in the sun here where there used to be an open-air pool
　　and once a Red Cross fete. There's the old air-raid shelter.
Front gardens mainly tarmacked, but privet and laburnum
　　and a Boeing to welcome me back to the semi in the cul-de-sac.
Everything seems as it was, even a boy racer's thunderbeat
　　feels meant for me, every immigrant face that of family.

IV

No surprise. It's where you were raised, the lost orchard.
　　What you're looking for is close, is coming out to reach you
and it's surely not coincidence you stand like a boy engulfed
　　by the joy of jet engines at your old house, identifying
ways to take to the air again—to pursue that contrail
　　this great monster overhead has lain as it lumbers its way
off to the Rhine or Como or further across the Med
　　and up the Nile to Lake Nasser, shooting all the Cataracts
to the Rift Valley, the Indian Ocean, even Zanzibar.
　　Yet, red door that I see in dreams so brightly,
you'd say it's home I'm looking for, the winking landing light

that passes over Prospect Close, the cinder Backway
(hear that old Lexicon card riffling my spokes),
   the Pit, the Sarsen Stone, and the woods at Cranford, secret
yew glades where I made movies, exposed the ghost
   of a stately home, and especially Heathrow: to play on the lifts,
or in the Queen's Building, looking for tail and wing, for exotic
   livery and fruit machines, happy prisoner of my teens.

V

They'll take me in. This is the sound of my earliest childhood.
   Hearing it, it triggers all kinds of half-forgotten instincts.
Yet they are undiminished—in some ways more potent than ever.
   Such treasures, the suns come bursting from the fruit machine.
Yes, the old things are here, an orchard where apples still hang
   but no one is going to pick them, this paradise remains.
And best of all is the discovery of what's been kept safe
   beneath the insulated loft, the rainbow wallpaper,
that reduces me to idiocy. Sheer delight. Another day, then,
   we can go and look at where the garden used to be,
the loganberry cordons, one Spring Bank Holiday, when Dad
   is at home, we can talk about all that's happened and it will come back.
I've weighed up many things since those days and for too long
   have said nothing about my spiritual cultivar, first set
in Heston, Chamberlain's paper airfield, the birthplace of English
   music's most famous unknown, and the source of Elizabeth's
sweet communion manchet; it's time to summon more than
   the metal angels of Heathrow—the immortal ones, and one

VI

I first divined in this house in those early years, whose roof
   was torn off by a plane one night, open in a moment
of renewal and glory to the music of the spheres. As if you could hear
   Hark the Herald broadcast from our candleless piano, scattered
by Mum's fingers across the neck of the banjo to our neighbours,
   inviting them to a secular Christmas, to this essence of family.
As we sit round the table and my father is not like a drunk
   in his diabetic hypo, who should I say thank you to?
Is it God, is there a God? If there is, isn't this too trivial

for Him to care about? Isn't this in the suburbs of His concerns?
It might be better to be silent, we don't have adequate language,
    make the most of this time between flights, leave the heart to beat.
Yet the right kind of music, the right words, might perhaps
    please or draw a response from skies clogged with ash
that allow presences to draw closer. If we do this,
    the sacrifices that lie under every holidaymaking runway
shouldn't shudder—like it or not, poetry has to absorb
    such painful undertones, internalise them, and let the rest fly.

The Interpretation of Owls

*Four owls on a branch, and one on its own, all smoking long churchwarden clay pipes,
and listening to the music of a nightingale in front of a giant moon—like five patients
waiting for wise Dr Freud.*

The First

Below me is a field
alive with khaki mice
not expecting to be killed.

Something else has risen,
so I keep one eye closed,
think back, and listen.

The Second

With most efficient clay,
and smartest plumage, I
will be ready for the day,

you miserable things.
Our tree may be scarred
but that young flapper sings.

The Third

I will not be swallowed
by light. My churchwarden,
elongated and hollowed

to amplify my dreaming
truths, remains silent
about all the screaming.

The Fourth

I've given up, except
to say: your call.
Yes, my pipe has drooped.

I would confess to nights
of hooting wild, but not
while she hits such heights.

The Fifth

No room on the branch,
yet I can see what they
and she cannot, the launch

of a future into your blue
unknowing. Of all that's yet
to come. To it, to you.

I found this untitled picture (reproduced on the book jacket and as the frontispiece) among my father's papers after his death. It is rather damaged, and in the lower right-hand corner are the initials CMG, with a partially visible date. My father had labelled the picture: "Drawn and painted by Clarence [Melville] Greening in 1901". If the date is correct, my grandfather would have been fifteen. It's not impossible he copied it, but Grandpa was a versatile and original caricaturist whose other drawings have just this same brand of humour. JG

Listening for Nightingales

All the birds of the dusk
sound beautiful. Is there one
that sounds true, that empties

a dark jug drunkenly
as Grafham Water raises its
H_2O? Ah, Keats

I envy you your certainty.
I too would fly by nightingale
if I could be sure that that

that's like a spring stuttering
out of a broken pipe were the pure
original song, and not

a drug on the market. Such black
burdens the wings of my enchantment,
it plunges off the green grid

and there is nothing. That magic
flew with your age,
and leaves me in the dark with mine.

Poets

She hangs her head there on the quiet fringes,
and has no voice now if she ever had,
but contemplates her egg. The many changes
have left her safe but solitary, glad
of this rough nest. The others don't get far—
a curlew curls his note of distant loss,
the gulls make drunken chorus at the bar
and warblers try short lyrics. Round the house,
the whistling, chirping, clicking nameless ones
are fed—until, somehow, beneath the gate,
in black and white, a creature who disdains
mere song is on the hunt for easy meat . . .
But she will not be moved. She'll guard for them
this gift of music from Byzantium.

Achill Island

Superheroes

Fieldfares in their superhero capes come hopping
about the front garden, masked and wary, but hoping
we'll keep the secret even as we stand here dropping

date-expired dried fruit and almonds. To be honest,
we took them for mild-mannered thrushes, would never have guessed
Batman or Bruce Wayne (or Robin) were there—but trust

The Birdlife of Britain (which Prince Charles claims to keep
not only in his car but 'on the bridge of my ship')
and, failing that, Google. Occasionally birds slip

off their own radar: that kingfisher once,
and—yes—the hummingbird I confidently announced.
It was a hummingbird moth. Forgive our ignorance,

and yet I do believe in birds. They come when they're called
by poets, too, tap-tapping at the screen. And I'm told
ornithoscopers were useful to heroes of old.

from Huntingdonshire Codices

A Wood Pigeon

How does that wood pigeon manage to stay on the delicate
hair trigger tip of our silver birch, our world tree?
So self-importantly placed, so sleek and pompous and fat,

he ignores the small birds' clamour for grub or crust
or crumb but enjoys a good view of all the millionaires
of Huntingdonshire: each new house bigger than the last—

forever upsizing, like post-*glasnost* Russian dolls.
Wind from the Urals shivers birchwhite to a ghost
of black canons with fish ponds and cony holes

and lynchet strips of twenty pigeon-tempting acres
and darker potences of squabs in dreadful concentration.
But the century calls: take flight, an away break

to the park or any extravagant Fen-trotting journeys,
keeping an open-all-hours mini milk bar
in his personal crop, pecking at those of others to earn his

award of Pest Status. He keeps his head high
and applauds himself as he leaves, offering one leisurely
coo! to the rest of the world's thin, wavering cry.

from Huntingdonshire Elegies

Geese

The in-formation
technology
of geese

can hear on its
high white
cirrus fibres

when the cold
is coming. Long
distance calls

awaken me each
morning. I lift
my head and let

the programmed
weatherline
croak on, watching

slack coils
of wire
stretch until

the message is
communicated,
then nestle

back to snore
snugly like
a warm receiver.

Clinton, New Jersey

Flight Into

You rise and the landscape opens beneath you.
Everything seems possible. Problems
reduce to tiny nothings. The overall
progression becomes clear. You are able
to map the outlines of your existence.

Then you sink. Slowly at first. Blue
gives way to the grey miasma of fact.
Cloud remoulds itself into something bricklike.
Faces appear where there was birdsong. The bump
as you hit the earth is like that moment you step

on the scales and feel the indicator clunk
up to reality. Your expectations are no more
than a colourful bag full of emptiness
which now collapses around you. You are
alone with a wicker basket, ballast, gas.

24th February 2013

But on the West Bank the ghosts of those
who thought they would enjoy
a balloon flight over the land of the dead

are wondering where they are now
as they wander the remains of Medinet Habu
or through the tomb-robbers' village

or pass the Colossi, still silent
as the sun rises, and find they have come
to the Valley of the Kings. We know the heat

but we lack the fabric to lift us out
of our doubts and away from the bones and dust,
to pass the dams and find the Mountains of the Moon.

27th February 2013

The first poem was written two days before news came of a balloon accident near Luxor in which nineteen people died. JG

The R101 Airship

Encounters with a ghost ship in Hyde Park,
witnesses who speak to the cameras of a scraping
at their chimney pots, the red and green lights

spooking a mushroom field, the lovers fumbling
for last minute protection . . . Behind celluloid,
champagne, cigars, intelligent conversation

about anything but the folly of all this—
leave that to those plimsolled labourers
prowling the catwalks, while the oil pressure

drops, the gas pressure drops, and the first
engine of the five predictably stops
over Hastings, into the dark night of la Manche.

from Gascoigne's Egg

Airfields

Widescreen, to *Gone with the Wind* themes, the Spaldwick road
slow-pans you towards forgotten footage. You spot the odd barn,
a token hawthorn butt, and countless anonymous farm tracks—

but the tracks are too straight, harder than they need be.
Each barn, as you make your approach, becomes a corrugated hut.
The road unreels its title sequence but your senses are enmeshed

by the foulness of brussels, silage, or is it that dead hare
you swerved to avoid? You do not expect to find living things out here.
No house for miles and, apart from the bird scarers, bird noise

would be the only sound if you were to wind down the glass: peewits'
low-level, high-volume aerobatics, or the viffing of skylarks—
like two half-witted, crack-voiced veterans of the old hundred:

make a joyful noise unto the Lord of Air-space! And so it fell
that half a century ago Dwight Eisenhower sowed the bulldog's teeth.
But there was no Golden Fleece; only, somewhere over the rainbow,

the Rhine ablaze. Now, occasionally, in the summer, a coachload
of balding shades will pause on its way to the Madingley graves to hear
that this is the village where Clark Gable's suits were tailored

and none will be told the uncanny tale that the village keeps and
does not advertise: the local man who was up and out early jogging
the broken runways: who saw what he saw, which is said to have been . . .

but secrets are what the Spaldwick road keeps best: the mist
encloses them more surely than the perimeter wire seals Molesworth's lips.
Unnumbered aircrew must have left from here. Some perhaps returned.

from Huntingdonshire Eclogues

Odyssey

Huge wide screen. *Thus Spake . . . 2001:*
A Space Odyssey—that school trip we made
when I was fourteen, voyage from the sun
out to farthest consciousness, a parade
of life's possibilities that had begun
for me with the Apollo programme and played
The Blue Danube and *Atmosphères* throughout
my teenage years. I'd been an astronaut

since watching how my last heroic crew
of single figures burnt up like those nine
birthday candles, too near the sun. I knew
where I must aim: her doppelgänger shine
each morning or each evening, warm and blue
and wrapped in cloud, impenetrably mine.
A Saturn Five would boost me there, away
from childish things, to love's half-year of day.

That mission was aborted. Skies turned red.
We moved back from the light. Our TV screens
began their nightly shower of wounded, dead,
fragments spun where a planet once had been,
destruction circling us. Yet in my head
I dreamed soft landing, peaceful dusty green
from melting icecaps, lichen, lost canals, dunes
to play in, a comforting pair of moons.

And now I look up from an easy chair
and pick out one gas giant, perhaps two—
a guilty red spot or a halo there.
It all seems so far off. I am not who
I was then at that Cinerama, where
a trinity of beams above me threw
incarnate mysteries of light and space
from a source blinding for a child to face.

Apollo

I'm in a hurry, sweeping through
oil, prohibition, sunken bullion,
trying to ignore those cheesy numbers
from the atrium, their Sunday lift-off,
so I almost miss the real show:

This is Houston—or more precisely,
Austin, the Bullock Museum, but still
the anchor controlling so much
drama in my own space age
when *Apollo* was the only god.

And at the word, Marsyas, droning
down in the lobby, lays his Texas
instruments aside, flayed to silence,
and white-haired, blue-shirted
Dave Heath reaches a hand.

He holds an iPad in the other,
for demonstrating the guidance system
he helped design that brought mankind
to earth after its lunatic giant
leap. Through jet lag

I try to process what I'm shown:
the shot of Dave in Mission Control,
the big-as-a-sideboard computer,
the mock-up of the moon's surface
where he stands to let my phone express

its appreciation of how the entire
programme could have been run from just
one of the icons at his fingertips,
how Dave was there in time for the stroke
of thirteen, *Houston—we have a problem.*

Austin, me too—I have a flight
to catch, back to my heath, where once
I watched that landing, heard those words.

But Dave knows his trajectory,
his eighty-something years continue

to count back up from the moment
he saw the first command module
break through and blossom into
earthrise, parachuting safely
into that sea which is named history.

Gravity

As the space shuttle crawls through the streets of Los Angeles
(streets which have had four hundred trees cut down to make room)
moving like that cor anglais through Birtwistle's *Triumph of Time,*

a man named Baumgartner—hoping to become the most
famous living Austrian after the Governor of California—
steps from the capsule that's hanging from a sheer-as-strudel balloon

at a height of thirty-eight kilometres to break the sound
barrier and at least three records even as he threatens to spin
out of control and into Newton's apple heap. Brueghel's

Icarus might well wish he had lived in a later time
as the cameras film him from every angle and the parachute
opens and Baumgartner—cultivator of trees—descends into the desert.

14th October 2012

Flight

for Jane

'Osprey shall fold
His wings and bow
His head and kneel'
    Ted Hughes

Our daughters are about to fly back home
after the wedding; it is a fine morning
here in Shoreline, on the fringes of Seattle,
so we walk for a while among the clapboard.

You are the first to spot it, whatever it is—
a heron? No, some kind of bird of prey
gliding behind the fir trees, perching on
a cell-phone tower. The man in the pickup

tells us what we are looking at and his word
signals more than I could have imagined
from the eye of that Loch whose wrinkles have spread
in sixty years beyond our smallest county

and even catches a white-feathered splash-
and-grab on the Nile ferry, dark-shawled
Nubian mothers balancing their babies, their baskets
of fruit and sighing. 'Osprey!' I wanted to say

as the bird with a fish in its claws carved its sign
on our yellow wall of heat. But you weren't there.
And now a pair of them, their high calling, over
Echo Lake and us in this littered garden.

America

Airmail for Chief Seattle

'Let him be just and deal kindly with my people, for the dead are not powerless.
Dead, did I say? There is no death, only a change of worlds.'

Recalling how in our English hurry
to 'stand in line', to go and bury
American hatchets, we took that ferry
in '99 out to the island,
your burial place, I fall silent
and shuffle towards the check-in salient.

Sixteen years. Before the cancer's
white cellular advance
across our bloodline and its chances.
Before the towers, the fall, the raven
repeating *more*. A kind of heaven.
What world, Seattle, do you live in?

That day I had the one mission
and one bus to the reservation
to show our children your lost nation.
Instead, I think they rather lost me.
Your words confronting death possessed me.
Death. I cannot put it past me.

And meanwhile, we have to live it.
We carry on and try to laugh it
off—a 'change of worlds'? I love it!
If only you had perhaps expanded,
we could approach the scan unhounded
by fears: what if all this ended?

It's time to tap into your knowing
cloud again. We've finished queuing.
Security's through. We'll soon be flying,
baggage free: the tunnels beckon,
the door, the smile, the seat not taken,
a smooth ascent, this sudden sicken-

ing plunge: an air canoe, shooting
rapids, in slow motion, fighting
nothingness, passengers courting
hollywood, i-power, the electronic
tundra, and stifling oceanic
yawns of fear. Don't panic.

It's time for me to write this letter.
On either side a grown-up daughter
and here, their mother. The pitter-patter
of tiny keys as I carve a totem
posting. Should I start at the bottom
or aim high? Dear Atom-

Splitter-in-Chief, forgive me prying,
but do you not remember saying
that when our children's children are playing
and think themselves alone, the shadow
spirits will come to them, that the dead are . . .
What precisely was your credo?

A child of Hounslow Heath, I conjured
paleface friends to get an injun
scalping in our garden, urged on
by PanAm drumrolls, feathers, warpaint,
'let's pretend'. Even Dick Turpin's
night flight was impotent

to hold us up, our timeless, rootless
idea of prairie: to fly footloose
from suburbs, ululating outlaws.
And yet it's not as if your people
were on our radar. The Bramley apple
above my head was home. That couple's

wigwam of runner beans. The tribal
elders of my sacred land who kindle
a bonfire, beat a cake, dwindle
to nothing below me as we leave the heathen
childhood backways, leaping our hawthorn
hedge, the mayflower; and find another

kind of world. Is this your answer?
Icefields, smoke, a glacier, a geyser,
a change of flights where people dance
away the darkless nights all summer
and keep the ghosts for winter, the murmur
of *huldufolk*, Odin, a rumour

of Spirit Guides. I came, following
my father's death, looking for Valhall,
a camp where he spent his war trawling
the ether for U-boats, and didn't
talk, but sensed perhaps the hidden
explosive depths. He would have trodden

respectfully the razor lava
you could walk with ease, lover
of the claw, the red tooth, believer
in magic. Is it this you inhabit
when not steaming through the carpet
at Microsoft or Boeing? The cockpit

has a new voice: we're cruising
etcetera, but what I'm raising
goes higher still. People are dozing.
So shift those plates and let your shaman
secrets flow: play me
that change of worlds. Or will it scare me

as much as this weird passage over
Greenland, Baffin Bay, a cove
or lake, waste that goes on for ever?
I'm ready to make the right connections,
to say that it's like when that white taxi
brought my friend to the funeral, tricksily

stepping from an ad for Icelandair
as a short-circuit in my mother's wiring
caused her doorbell to start *whirring* . . .
And no answer on Bainbridge Island
that day we came to you from England
to visit what had been your own land,

'a place of clear still water' stretching
below us now. We change direction.
Unplug my ears. There, crouched
on grass beside your grave (a dreamwork
of dug-out timbers, a mythic framework)
we saw SEALTH, and headed homewards.

Sixteen years since then. Our girls are
savvy smartphone users (the wheels
go down), their past a fading pulsar
full of messages. A sense of falling
back and forwards. Silently calling
(an ancient device), I catch a smiling

face in the cloud, a wrinkled mountain,
wink from a lake, a shadow hunting
over forest and freeway now haunting
its own grounded self, but nothing
from your side. The door, scything,
releases us, our breathing.

Mowing

after Robert Frost

No sound but the heated throb of a mower,
and nothing in my head but a tick of fear
as cogged eyes clock the three long hours of lawn.
But what this whirring locust can't devour
is mind, that keeps leaping up to woods where deer
emerge at dusk to browse in people's yards
and leave among the clippings Lyme Disease,
against which leaflets in the library warn.
The blade throws mothwings, poppyseeds and shards
that flash and could be Indian artefacts—
except I mustn't dream. Shadows in trees
might make a bull's-eye of me, or a slow
unnerving of my scalp, but not distract
me from the long straight lines I need to mow.

On Chief Tamenund's Mountain

for Mike Petrus

An empty Bud Light
dropped where the leaves
are dropping these last
days of September.

Taking it by the scruff
of its plastic cross,
you curse the bastard
who let it fall—

but then catch the feel
of another, wilder shape
in your hand: one stone
picked from others

identical, only this
hurled into the heart
of a black bear or used
to tear at its hide.

You trail the throwaway
down to where the cars
and the trash cans are,
but keep in your bag

(trees lumbering into
blackness, towards bareness)
that permanently sealed
vision of a lost way.

Delaware Water Gap

Good Friday in the 'Please Touch Museum', Philadelphia

The gates invite us to reach out our hands
and touch, for a clutch of silver to suffer
all day the little children. Swaddling bands
tighten on parents. An hour is enough
of a good thing on Good Friday. Dear Christ,
when I was no father I kept such faith
in days like this. Now I make the mere best
of common ignorance. Death is just death
and I've no desire to go touch its wounds,
happy to watch kids push, pull, squeeze, swipe, stroke
without being lectured, their natural sounds
breaking on my holy driftwood. Yet who
could leave the City of Brotherly Love
and live in this padded cell? God above . . .

Fall, 1990

I

The 'sycamore' above Norman's Eatery
must come down one of these days,

its roots are internal organs spilling
from the town's high water defences

where widows hover and the wasps ask
for honey bagels. The river is eating

sky anemones and starfish of the air
in preparation for a long assault.

It must come down, though the fig leaf
of a Biblical misnomer remain.

II

The Red Mill is only a museum now
but the waterfall continues to rise

and threaten flood in all Main Street
from Norman's through the antique emporium

to *Dove Hollow*. No more revolutions
of the rusty wheel, but the children

of veterans dive there and their fathers
show off white-water skills, while others

unprotestingly sit beside a fishing pole
or jog past with weights in their clutch.

III

Above, the geese make one melancholy
departing V of each of their calls

and, with the fire department's rallying
wail, put out the summer.

There is a yellowing ribbon on every tree
except on that one plane which is too fat

and in its mottled camouflage resembles
General Schwarzkopf distinguishing between air

superiority and air supremacy and refusing
to get into the business of body counts.

Clinton, New Jersey

Once Upon Route 22

I jangled along the shoulder
without bearings, halfway
between Bridgewater and home

stuck on three wheels
in a career, not even middle-
aged yet, overtaken by

Oldsmobiles. As a tornado
sweeps through Oklahoma
destroying an entire school,

a thought gathered and rose
darkly towards the turnpike
but turned at once into

Dan, his two bright
sidelights winking and blinking
me back to where my daughter

skipped between gravestones
to nursery school, making it
just in time for ever after.

Lullaby for Charles Augustus Lindbergh Jr.

Hushaby baby
                        in your maplewood nest
When the wind blows
                              the world seems at rest
When the news breaks
                             the headlines will drop
On front lawn
                  and front porch
                             and doormat
                                       and stoop

Hushaby Charlie
                    your Daddy's come home
When the wind blows
                          the trees make their moan
When the rung cracks
                          the kidnapper's gone
From Hopewell
                 New Jersey
                         and Flemington Town

Hushaby Lindbergh
                    alone in your room
When the wind blows
                        your nursemaid will come
When her smile fails
                 the curtain will fall
On nursemaid
                and mother
                       and father
                           and all

'Lullaby for Charles Augustus Lindbergh Jr.' is taken from my verse drama about the Lindbergh kidnap, A Ladder in Hopewell, which was written in 1991 during our stay in New Jersey, not far from the Flemington Courthouse, where Richard Hauptmann's trial had taken place in 1935. The play was first staged in Asheville, North Carolina, in 2002 by Jericho Productions, directed by Franklin Harris. JG

Sibelius in America

He looks at the Horseshoe Falls, the American Falls and is lost for words
as the *Maid of the Mist* sails round and round. If he could only convey it . . .
But no, it is too solemn and vast for painter, composer or poet.
It outreaches humanity. It plays unhearable, unbearable chords,

repeating and repeating in its thundering undertones simplicity, modesty,
as the man in the white flannel suit, unspeaking, boards a ship
for home; and passes icebergs, and hears how a certain Princip
shoots the Archduke. Behind him, caviare, acclaim, supremacy.

Falls

1. DIVES: *Sam Patch*

The name is Sam. I'm twenty-two.
Dream up a dive for me to do.

I leap wherever the rainbow calls.
Today I jump the Horseshoe Falls.

Patch is the name. The first who dived:
twice I fell, and twice survived.

But the third was the one that made my name:
drowned in the syndicated rapids of my fame.

2. TIGHTROPE: *Blondin*

Diving is nothing. But paying out a hawser,
cable-laid, three inches in diameter,
thirteen hundred dollars long, to span Niagara,
Blondin the Great has come.

Paying is nothing. But to stretch manila fibres
taut, from America's Pleasure Grounds to Canada,
fasten them with eighteen guyropes, admit the world for
twenty-five cents each.

To boast is nothing. But to step on to that cable,
walk halfway and drop a bottle on a string to
crowds below, then up and drink the contents,
cheers, and off again.

To walk is nothing, but to run along the tightrope,
somersault, in darkness, on stilts, or do it backwards,
blindfold, in irons, on a bicycle, or once even
pushing a wheelbarrow.

To impress is nothing, but to leave the watchers speechless,
carrying a stove out to the centre, cracking eggs and
cooking a perfect omelette, eating it, then lowering
portions to pleasure boats.

To be famous is nothing, but to be preserved on camera
carrying one's manager across, and recorded offering
piggybacks to a Prince, His Royal Highness whispering:
Thank God that's over!

To be a stuntman. Nothing. But—to be Blondin.
Retire to an English estate and title it 'Niagara',
die in your bed at the far end of a full span:
the greatest of all stunts.

3. MAID OF THE MIST

Don't think about after you've crossed the Falls:
Niagara Gorge, the rapids, where above
a man is walking tightrope with a stove
strapped to his back, and ahead there are calls
from a honeymoon couple caught when the walls
of their ice bridge collapsed. Just try to prove
the glory of this place is like true love,
indestructible . . . I'm over. My barrel's
about to smash down in Canada. When I'm
a shape (unnoticed by those blue-robed hordes
boarding their ferry to cross the wild Styx)
pinned under plunge and sensation and time,
tell that girl, the rainbow girl throwing me words
inflatable, kiss-shaped, I'm done with tricks.

4. BALLAD OF WEBB AND THE FERRYMAN

Why do you come here, Captain Webb,
  to court our rapids and pool?
You've swum the Channel, you've made your name,
  people will say you're a fool.

I come to swim, O Ferryman,
  because it's a summer's day,
because I'll have two thousand suns
  in my bank account today.

O spend it, spend that money, sir,
  before you leave my boat:
those rapids will pick you pocketless,
  that whirlpool will slit your throat.

I come to swim, O Ferryman,
  the currency of obsession.
Goodbye, my boy, the hourglass calls,
  I am in true love's possession.

O Captain, leave your life-saving medal
  and leave your wife the proof
that they promised you two thousand dollars
  if you could swim it and live.

For the Ferryman knows you won't return
  and the railroad men don't pay.
He sees you caught in your own limbs' web
  and the widow whirls you away.

5. THE BARREL: *1901, Annie Edson Taylor*

Annie Edson Taylor is lost for words
as they lobotomise her padded barrel
and help her out. She has fallen over the lip
of the century, down the hundred years to our
snug armchairs where we now look at her

shaken, haggard face. Today she is forty-six:
a teacher's birthday outing shooting the Horseshoe
Falls into the first Brownie box camera,
the first radio transmission, and Freud's
Interpretation of Dreams. Men's arms reach out

to her, this lonely widow, who so needed
support she was prepared to climb between these hoops
of fame, only to find the fruit long gone,
to find herself alone on stage in a dust bowl,
and now, beside her barrel, hawking penny dreams

to those whose dream was gold: sexlessly grinding how
she rode those seventeen minutes to the edge,
her fall into oblivion, and a lifetime
waiting for the crash—bob! bob! bob!—gravid
with awe and such passion she could only utter:

Nobody ought ever to do that again.

6. FALLS

We all go over the Falls,
Survive or don't survive

The seven year old whose toy
boat whistles him from the sink

The fourteen year old whose dare
cuts out and sheers to the brink

We all go over the Falls,
Survive or don't survive

The twenty year old whose girl
sprays mist till he drifts too far

The thirty year old whose wife
drops buoys where the hazards are

We all go over the Falls,
Survive or don't survive

The forty and fifty year olds
whose jobs are padded and cooped

The sixty year olds who finish
more famously than they'd hoped

We all go over the Falls,
Survive or don't survive

The seventy year old life
that flashes in spectral spray

that seven year old whose dream
boat whistled you from your play

We all go over the Falls,
Survive or don't survive

'Falls' was written at the request of composer Paul Mottram, whose setting was premiered by the Dunedin Consort at Wigmore Hall, London, June 2000. JG

78

When it was *Whispering Grass*
on one side and *Maybe*
on the other at seventy-eight
revolutions per minute
you had to lower a thorn
into a shellac groove.

Today, the Ink Spots
are Spotified, and Lady
Gaga spins her live
nightingale anthem from
a sacred grove of flags
before the Capitol.

That disc was cracked
and scratched, but I kept
on playing it. Why tell us
all of the old things?
Anything but a forty-five.
It's snowing on the Mall.

Washington Crossing

The Delaware, Christmas Eve, 1776

We are crossing it unaware
    towards the Mall
    and last minute gifts

A headline: Man drowned
    rescuing dog from ice
    in Central Park today

Seven presents, each one of
    the seven mirrors, mirages
    or veils

Here, some of that fresh ice
    kept deep in the earth
    all summer at Sulgrave

Is that a sliver of the Berlin
    Wall, that shiver
    as the globe warms

Now on sale, the art
    of distilling moonlight—
    wink away depression

Glaciers, too, launder past
    as they advance
    on their own extinction

Then, techno-wizardry, each unique
    crystal screen
    showing CNN

Oranges from California
    unfrosted, innocent
    of blackness

Non-vegetarians and pro-choice
    may care to visit us
    upstairs

Crossing the line
    our dreams ice up, the last
    Dresden shepherdesses fired

Refrigerators packed full
    of date-stamped perishables
    shudder, groan

O what is this land
    where vines grow undefoliate
    you frost giants

South versus North, poles
    apart, both caps ice-cold,
    both molten at the core

Store entrances and sewer
    gratings are still the hottest
    Broadway seats

Iceland, says this old
    English geezer, it's like
    everywhere, full of Yanks

No cold like the cold
    of a November widow
    in her limousine

Gods of world war, guard
    the secret combinations to
    your locked freeways

Katie in a Prospect of D.C.

Outside the Oval Office
my daughter started
to sing Humpty Dumpty.

Then, at a rising black wall
that dropped to a V,
she stopped singing and cried

for a flag of stars
to wave past the dark
windows of the Space Museum.

On Capitol Hill, she
chattered towards a life-
size image of Jesus,

was silent before the statue
of the Father of Television,
heard the floor whisper.

But approaching Watergate,
she pressed her investigative nose
to the glass, and broke in

on our conversations again
and again to report
what all the king's men couldn't.

Natural History

Like all the others here, my daughter,
my wife, and I are looking for
the Hope Diamond. A shuffling

Sunday of similar noses, up
against *cat's eye, adventurine,*
glossed but improbable names

by which to distinguish the real thing.
I, however, am distracted by a globe
on the farther side, displayed

most plainly, the plain crystal
ball of myth and fairy tale—
apparently, the world's largest.

I watch it, using television skills,
for some unconscious, prophetic shape,
but see, of course, nothing. Not even

myself, only a risky feeling.
My family, meanwhile, have identified
the famous thing, which is blue

and cut by convention to a distant
cold adornment. Unmoving,
but for the ill wind that stirs

legend—how that millionairess,
fearing for her child and for her stone,
kept both under armed guard, till

one slips out with a delivery van
and is killed on the road. We separate.
The two I love entering a dark

gallery of phalloids, snatches
from Fingal's Cave, meteorite
droppings, moon rock; I, to look

again into that crystal, never
cut, but lovingly, secretively
polished through months' and years'

desire . . . Go, family, drifting on
where the glass-eyed beasts gaze
out through glass from a seamless

artifice of property and paint—
the endangered, the extinct, and await me
where you see a horned triceratops.

Rosie in a Retrospect of D.C.

This little toon
that giggles from the depths
of her sleep, flicking
muscles in dream joy

was less than a cel
until we came
to Washington in a hot
June three years ago

to catch up with the Air
and Space and touch
moon rock and stand
beneath that battered

myth of Apollo,
visiting all monuments
to the word shot—
and it was hot

where she was conceived,
while the pumpkins
flowered in the dry yard
and the cicadas

wound their reels in
from the night, and we
were hooked on the
Little Mermaid video.

Sea Urchins

Cape Ann, Massachusetts

We have trampled
those delicate
eggs of the night,
the sea urchins,

fragments of a dream
extravagance caught
when the moon
went off and the sea

turned over. Now,
attending to
the Dry Salvages,
they drift before

my eyes as rock
music slumps
across the bay
like polythene.

In the bladderwrack
at my feet, oil,
aerosol, syringe
and one whole lightbulb.

Tonight the moon,
a Beethoven CD,
will inspire
our child's first poem—

I like the way
it shines over the sea
that's because
it's me—and I

have picked a small
and perfect
urchin, remembering
when I was small

the one my parents
brought home from
the seaside
made into a lamp.

Mayflower: Three Expeditions

for Cecilia McDowall

Our first expedition
is over land, around a creek and through a forest
to where we find a spring and a reed basket
of dried corn, yellow, red and blue.
A thousand beady eyes stare up at us.
We take the corn.
The first fruit of the *Mayflower*.

Our second expedition
takes us across the bay into a little ice age
and under it the grave of a European sailor,
his skull with its blonde hair, his knife, his needle.
We open our eyes on to a great span of snow.
Cold Harbour we call this.
The first blossom of the *Mayflower*.

Our third expedition
is into Thievish Harbour where we carry our beads
in sign of peace, until the cries come and the arrows
Woath! Woach! Ha! Ha! Hach! Woach!
fifty to a quiver, firing faster than any musket,
five together in the air.
The first thorns of the *Mayflower*.

Wounded Knee

A noise like the tearing
of the world's biggest blanket—

the one that our holy man told us
would roll up all the fences,

railroads, mines and telegraph poles
and underneath would be our

old-young Indian earth
and the whole of our lost family

and we would be invulnerable
if we would only put on

our ghost shirts and dance
the ghost dance in the snow

that Christmas. A noise like
the tearing of the world's

biggest blanket. But Black
Coyote cannot hear it—deaf

before they even start to shout
at him to give them his rifle.

Now he dances like the others,
like that young mother,

her baby still at the only
centre it had known

and on its head a cap
of beads in the pattern

of the Old Glory.
The blizzard freezes

the motionless formation
the senseless design

into the limbs
of a fallen sacred tree

into the pieces
of a nation's broken hoop.

Seattle

Bezelled, faceted ridge—
like a printout at the foot
of a hospital bed.

Seattle cannot see it,
he is laid out
with a hopelessly broken tribe.

White men come around
with their accoutrements
and their potlatch: we

will be transferring you
to a more convenient place
afterwards, they say,

they need his bed,
they need his agreement,
the name of his next of kin,

offering a quiver of pills
and a tube to breathe
peace through, peace,

removing the oxygen tepee,
the totem drip, masked
for the scalp dance.

Chihuly

It is to be born into a fragile garden
between today's rain and my left brain

where the artist hangs like one of these
colourful characters with nowhere to go

around the Space Needle, shooting up
while thickets of spike, globe, prong, whorl

induce a Laocoön, a Medusa, a phant-
asmagoria of primary gasps

and shapes theatrically bold, the set
for a drama of some deep unscripted delta

breathing all its heat and wind into
grey or-have-you-ever-been grey

Pacific Northwest, a frozen moment
of bright translucency that seizes

Venice, the Citadel of David, and,
with one closed eye, an open Palm

House where (on cue) my future grew
shining, rosy, at the end of the tube.

A Feather

'Like dropping a feather
into the Grand Canyon
and waiting for the echo,'
I said of my first book
to my mother's friend
who had survived Auschwitz,
but watched her family
taken and processed by its
barbaric machinery.

We were talking in the garden
on that suburban lawn
in Eastcote, where nothing
serious had ever happened
and even Boeings did not
bother to intrude. Ruth
worked with my mother
in the histology lab, where they
were diagnosing cancer.

The last time we met her
was on the roof of the World
Trade Center, full of our
first child, a coming second,
my poetry. She talked—
of what? Another canyon
opens there, the vultures'
high whining, and up from
the dust, a death fugue.

The Seven

'The executive order announced on Friday suspends entry to the US for all refugees for 120 days . . .'
     The Guardian, *January 2017*

In Persepolis, at the Gate of All Nations,
they climb the dual stairway, huddled masses.

From Nimrud, colossi haul their wingless burden
of art and thought and learning, towards America.

At Leptis Magna, the ghost of Severus decrees
the people may go, he has had enough of walls.

Out of Dhambalin's caves, the colour flies
from painted figures, their dream of a white pirate.

Among the pyramids of Kush, a black pharaoh
raises himself to bless the inundation.

Through the Arch of Triumph at Palmyra, the dead
march with stones in their hands on passport control.

Shibam. Its towers, rising through dust as far as
Fifth Avenue, tell their billion stories.

Asylum

Athens, Ohio

An early morning walk through
the lunatic asylum's
lonely hilly grounds, up to
the Ridges, where I had thought
those birds following me were
eagles (but they were vultures),
and I kept on coming round
to the same point. Ohio
is quiet. Memorial
Weekend. The cemeteries
are quieter still, along
the nature trail, old inmates
marked with small fluttering stars
and stripes, but nothing there for
such a wing-span, wide as this
blackness in my room where the
news keeps on rolling, circling.

November 2018

To Sir Walter Ralegh

How easily we press a button and the car unlocks for our drive
to Budleigh Salterton, how painlessly we buy a ticket and pass through
the barrier with the children for their day out at the Tower of London,
how thoughtlessly enter the tube that will fly us to Cadiz or Guyana

until a volcano erupts in Iceland and all flights from Europe are grounded
or a dispute about overtime meets a sticking point and a red signal
or a misjudgment near the Little Chef means slow cooking
in a twenty-mile queue. We take our freedom to travel for granted

as you did, before they threw you in prison for thirteen years:
a man of the world, impatient for the latest tour to promote
the brand, her image, your merchandise, new-fangled things
(potato, tobacco), by appointment. You always hated to walk,

but to sail into battle for booty, or to claim your patents, monopolies,
exotic wines and mines and Irish salmon fisheries,
until Bark Ralegh was transmuted—yes, you had the arts
of an alchemist, they all said—to Ark Royal. Now the Americas,

Virginia, a New-found Land . . . In all this, did you forget
your scallop shell of quiet? Was there a secret longing
for a retreat, a Walsingham, some lapping pebble beach in the west?
You found it in that corner of the Tower. And on your final journey

to the block, your head in a book. An American I met here
tells me he has no home, no fixed address, he shifts
like Yeats's tribesman: now a writing colony, next the apartment
of a friend. Fare forward, traveller. But how to stop,

to cope when the planes don't fly, the trains aren't running,
or our cars are all out of fuel? The oil-slick gushes
from the radio. The volcano spews. The wildfire strikes
spread and spread. What will we do with ourselves then, Wat?

We shall write our History of the World, perhaps, or find time
to read all those poems that have flowed since you lost your head
and make sense of it all. I am gazing out at the wall
of Drummond's castle. A bee probes the stone. He was a poet

who went nowhere. He wrote. Or invented telescopes, devices
for observing the strength of winds, for converting salt water
to sweet, for measuring distance at sea. Although up the road
it was fire and famine, the Covenanters pressing him to sign,

and war upon civil war, he would not leave Hawthornden:
to make a castle of one's life, to condemn the bold spirits
(as Popham and Manchester condemned you) to bar the door.
Then, the dream of escape. You believed you made it. But listen:

your Devonshire burr is ineradicable. Throw down your cloak
and let Her Royal Progress advance over the mud. The history
of the world is still not finished. Follow the cycleway
down the disused line to Newbattle. Then on to El Dorado.

A Letter to Mike Petrus

'the voices of my accursed human education'
  D. H. Lawrence

I think I'd like to find two mountain lions in my back yard.
We've had a muntjac, our cat once brought a baby rabbit,
the usual selection of shrews and voles and mice—oh, and both
varieties of woodpecker, neither of them as striking
as that one with the magic fez who pattered on unfazed
while you were pointing out the winter quarters of a moth
defoliating your woods, those tents of caterpillar
in full battle gear. That was my exchange year, when the Gulf
was ablaze, Bush remaining unsinged. And the day we saw
a black bear, as if the myth had broken from a cocoon
of longing and even left its droppings for us there, warm
proof that if you wish on something that isn't Disney, it
can star for you in a lost silent picture, and unreel
beyond the Special Relationship, beyond D-Day and trench
tea-parties and all mad German kings . . . But your lions came
'to exchange long looks at twenty yards in the morning light'
and took up residence (you write) in a place unconsciously
made ready for them, beside the creek, where the mowing ends:
pumas, cougars, panthers, painters, catamounts, living
not anthologised with the dead and fabulous, nor preserved
by Frost's gaze in gladiatorial applause, but to make
themselves at home even as they stay apart, like old friends.

A Letter from America

A friend from America emails, telling of wild fires
and White House fury. Curious relief that ours
is the soggiest, foggiest, least combustible of shires,

our *Bücherverbrennung* long since cold, grassed
over, a fading cropmark, a puritanical waste.
We're safe. And not to be cavalier, even the worst

would only provoke a shrug at this late date.
I think of my father: all those immaculate
rings made from the news laid so lovingly in the grate

for fifty years. I do the same. A poisonous wraith
of 2018 puffs from our Victorian hearth
as my reply to Santa Rosa takes a breath

to leap the gap between those sickly Wellingtonia
marching through our minor public school, and sequoia
standing up to whatever comes in California.

from Huntingdonshire Codices

Wartime

Barnes, February 26th, 2022

A 'Lion House'—she couldn't mask her pride,
although we saw she'd stuffed the *Morning Star*
inside the *Telegraph*. And then we had
that falling out about my books. There were,
she said, too many, endangering the floor.
She also made complaints about our bed.
To her we were intruders, newly wed.

Those lions still adorn the gate and roof
unmoved by forty-something years since we
lived childless, mortgageless. Hurrying off
to cross the common for the BBC
each day, where mostly I'd write poetry.
But Jane was in the Russian Service, where
she dealt with dissidents, was even there

when Markov (from the office next to hers)
was murdered with a ricin-tipped umbrella.
She too was on that bridge, passed through those doors
the day he died; they never caught the killer.
And I'd be talking music with Hans Keller,
a refugee himself, who knew the point
of dancing angels. The times were out of joint.

But aren't they still. We take our selfie, showing
a lamp post by our flat marked 007,
and lions rampant. Why return then, knowing
the worst was on the cards today in Kyiv?
Perhaps to make the most of what we have.
Some gains, I think, since 1978.
But roaring starts to shake the golden gate.

In Trafalgar Square

Among the forbidden pigeons, they have gathered
as in any other summer: the latest
security threat won't stop them, the weather
has gone on feeding them. They flutter requests

to have their picture taken at the paws
of Landseer's imperial colossi—less often
below that armless, legless, pregnant torso
and head that coos triumphantly at Nelson,

who turns his back on her, inspects his fleet
of lamp posts down the Mall. Can he see the queues
in Terminal One from there? Some top nob's sights
must be on war, but no one moves, unless

ascending the steps into the National
to catch the Embarkation of St Ursula,
check out a Flight into Egypt, or a flash
of pale-skinned Bathers. Art mocks Life and Terror

is *trompe l'œil*: so, go climb the plinth, adopt
a lion, and play I'm King of the Column,
waving to camera phones, or have yourself snapped
between two yellow-jacketed policemen.

August 2006

Tribute

At Fotheringhay, she's
thrown a swan's feather
into the Nene,
not to say 'coward',

not for those mute
numbers migrating
and breeding in Iraqi
airspace, but as her

tribute (like this
wreath here, freshly
laid, its ballpoint
message targeting

'murder') to the one
fragment that would not
be moved by a bullying
dynasty. It is still

February. The river,
however, is king
of spin and makes
my daughter's offering

an accusation, turning
a hunched back
away from us and
on to March

to advance in ruled
straight lines
towards the empire
of the Wash, her feather's

opinion, like her father's,
caught by the downing
thistlebeds and banks
of oil-stained bush.

February 2003

Mene Mene

The bomber wrote its message above Baghdad
and from its shadow something dark slipped
to explode in a cluster of clay tablets,
figurines, seals, pottery, tools.

The target, a secret arms factory,
was intact, but all around were bursting
friezes and faces, a ram from a thicket,
a gold harp, a dagger, a chariot

and coins, coins . . . Carefully guided
mythology from the third millennium before
Christ, lovingly crafted smart
technology from Ur, the war-games of Gil-

gamesh played by all those generals
in cuneiform in the history bunker, like Dudu
of Lagash, or Shalmaneser, or Belshazzar
safe behind the wall of Babylon HQ.

Hearts and Minds

Your days are programmed on a shining disc.
The moon locates us Babylon and Ur.
We click and move from task to aimless task.

The dusty screen before me is a husk
of sun rising from empire's fallen tower.
Your days are programmed on a shining disc

in cuneiform. What scholars now to ask?
The scarabs push their dung. The wise stay poor.
We click and move from task to aimless task.

The West End winks: come in and take the risk,
though every act's a theatre of war.
Your days are programmed on a shining disc.

I shut the *Times*, she stares into the dusk:
the privilege of peace. But on the hour,
we click and move from task to aimless task

as if through gas or virus, this one mask
against all barefaced rumours of a cure.
Your days are programmed on a shining disc.
We click and move from task to aimless task.

Ur

Like peeling Assyrian
from Sumerian
from Akkadian at Ur,

the search for Saddam's
biological and chemical
and nuclear weaponry.

UN Inspectors speak
of repeated evasions
and having to dig

past ululating ranks
of veiled women
banner-waving their

love of the father
of the mother of all battles.
Quiet American

inspectors video
his lapis beads
of uranium enrichment,

his chemical chains
of gold, his carnelian
bio-rosettes . . . and erase

those royal death-pits
where court ladies
curl in obedience

to their leader, cylinders
of poison at their side,
like Jonestown, like Waco.

Ur is in modern Iraq. During excavations in 1922, the body of a queen was discovered, buried alongside her attendants. This poem was written when the hunt was on for Saddam Hussein's weapons of mass destruction in 1997. Only after a later Gulf war was it established that he probably had few or none. JG

Ice Hockey in Time of War

A Midwinter Night's Game

Padded to look like men,
faceless, behind iron grilles,
and wielding sticks huge
as tactical battle equipment,
these dumb mechanicals swerve
across the ice and collide
with cheers from parents, packed
in front of hazy screens.

Every now and then a siren
goes off and the young
leave the arena like body-bags
while reinforcements are lured
on to the ice by a puck
that will reduce them all to asses.

Feast Day, Melchbourne

A yellow field for the cars to crawl into.
Moonlight Serenade from the Ouse Valley Band.
Tombola, bric-a-brac, a raffle, Pimm's
and ninepins, coconut shies and strawberries.

We seem to have drifted back to the last war
when Glenn Miller gave his final performance
on this lawn in front of the manor house.
And even as we scramble behind the tractor

for a ride out of the grounds, the sounds of
Perfidia and *American Patrol*
accompany us into the oilseed rape.
The farmer's boy, who's clinging to his trailer,

points through the bones of wych elm and thorn
and escalating nightshade to a chain-link fence
that flickers 'Danger Area' as we pass.
That's Coppice Wood, where they stored the mustard gas

for bombs. They tried to clear it in the fifties.
Thirty people a week were carted off
with burns. Abortions in cattle and sheep.
The air was black. His tractor turns to face

the slope where once the Knights Hospitaller
had their preceptory, before it was flattened
for baseball. When locals complained they were told
no way, there isn't nothing in the woods.

Our Fathers

One puts his Tiger Moth into a spin
over Niagara Falls. The other sits
in Akureyri with his headset and waits
for weather reports. Neither was really in
the war, saw Normandy beaches, felt his tin
helmet peppered; neither would ever fight.
Only boredom, bitterness. One on his night
watches, one preparing others to win
the air war. But had they not been sent
to Canada or Iceland, what of me
or you? We might not even now exist.
Two futures taken and violently bent
over Berlin or under the North Sea,
or broken in that land attack they missed.

Letter to My Father

It's hard to follow Auden, but a letter seems right:
to you in your Valhalla, from me looking for the site
of Valhall Camp. Can you believe they called it that—
a gift of pure irony for a poet here where poetry
is the national sport? I've thought about it for weeks, just why
I had to come, when you had always chosen to keep away.
Perhaps I'm simply gratifying chronic addictions:
physical geography, desert, ice, or my obsessions
with the second war and those unmarked contributions
my own father made to it—not forgetting the Edda,
the sagas, the mythology, the romance. And yet for you, Dad,
it was just a posting then; and later all you said
was 'the place is full of Yanks'. Now look again. It's not
full of anyone but *huldufolk*. Snorri's bath's still hot
after seven centuries, but they've hidden your old tin hut.
You surely must have loved this crystal clarity in the air,
the salt fish edge to the breeze; and have begun to share
feelings uncamouflaged by your concern with the war,
with spells of duty, fatigues, night watches and Morse
examinations. You never explored the culture. Old Norse
was a blank to you. You took a correspondence course
in journalism, wrote home, but I never heard you speak
of a saga, only cigarettes, of how you would smoke
your way through the long winter nights . . . and then the lack
of all things that a twenty-year-old might enjoy
except for walks, talks, unrationed food, football, a boys'
night out at the cinema . . . few girls (those 'stukas'), but noise
of laughter under the stars. Things which meant so much
years later that you always fought to keep in touch
with your old Iceland friends—who still strike a match
on the rainbow bridge, on shields of Valkyries, in their warm replies
to my enquiries: what they recollect . . . where Valhall was . . .
the flash of memory shimmering in blacked-out skies.

Night Watch

'And there in hope the lone night-watches keep'
    Cardinal Newman: 'The Dream of Gerontius'

His sixth long hour of listening, the door
bursts open on a sudden wind, an ash-
tree gnarled and split by darkness, the aurora's
unreeling war, and a figure in a hat
pulled low. The young recruit, unworried, turns
to meet the silence of an eye that can flash
only blindness, and one that arcs and burns
its quicksilver covenant, forged from slicks
of sunk convoys. Too late, he hears the sirens.
The riddles descend—

                What's six years long, six
continents wide, and six million dead?

He does not know, of course. The wireless clicks
unanswered. The questions roll, crash.

                         I'm red,
I brag and cry, tell lies, tear man from wife,
yet lead my passive children to be fed
in sweetest meadows of their father's life.
What am I?

           The boy looks round. He needs a clue
to how he should reply, some bland words safe
from censorship. But senses only two
ravens cruising free from the hut like flying
bombs towards his home. The adept recruit
shrivels beneath this blitz of *Who What Why*
and when he tries to shelter, disconnect,
Why does the God of War have one blind eye?
flattens him.
           Till dawn. Present and correct,
he rubs his eyes and is relieved. But life
has grown in ways that he did not expect.

Liber Scriptus

A tiny diary, red
with its red tail
still attached to mark a page—
the moon's phases, apothecaries'
weights, measures of space
or the date of winter solstice.

Each day inscribed in blue
from a fountain pen with all
the minutiae of Iceland life:
letters written and received,
books read, films seen,
the countdown to the June Boat.

That this has survived,
bought in Richmond, carried
on the *Champollion* to an un-
decipherable land and back
through years of waste paper
to be read by pixel-light

is astonishing. It is a glowing
lava bomb tossed from the war,
that grey unmoving six-year
flow that now smothers
the century. It is hot
and dangerous, a man's life.

from Iceland Requiem

Enigma Variations

He takes a bite out of the poisoned apple
and falls into oblivion. At your computer
you google Alan Turing: the green secret
begins its paring, red Englishness decoded
as he and others closeted in Bletchley
succeed in cracking Germany's Enigma.

But who will colour in this blank enigma?
Of those who were the first to taste the apple
among ten thousand pigeon-holed at Bletchley,
none knew they were inventing the computer,
none guessed they were a key to be decoded
themselves, perhaps a better feathered secret

than anything the Wrens sat on (*Top Secret*),
who now nest in a petrified Enigma
Machine of history's making, undecoded,
unable to confess they'd eaten apple
(the green, the red) except to their computer
or, sixty years on, flitting out to Bletchley

from caves where no wall ever echoed 'Bletchley',
to let the children know we know their secret,
that here we summoned it—some new computer
adventure they're addicted to: *Enigma*,
Colossus or *Station X*. An apple
whose bite has turned Socratic and, decoded,

spells Alan Turing. So much to be decoded,
refreshed, acknowledged. Here at sunny Bletchley
Park fruit is swelling. Tree takes back its apple,
admits paternity, blurts out the secret
pollinating power-buzz of Enigma,
its bombes, ripe, orotund. In each computer

hard drive are pigtails, plaits, a young computer
rooting for its terminal, the drum-encoded
dream of at last deciphering enigmá-
tic whirring from hacked hedgerows even Bletchley
ignored: the core, the pre- and post-war secret
unsolved since birds first pecked the human apple.

An apple fell beneath Hut 8 at Bletchley,
its seed not yet decoded; a computer
receives its secret mating call: *enigma*.

Ballad of the B-17

'Groß ist der Männer Trug und List'
   Eichendorff

The gunner lay beneath his girl
   and gazed beyond her eyes.
He saw the constellations wink
   clear warning from the skies.

Tomorrow you will fly, they said,
   your twenty-fifth and last.
Back home then, and back down to earth:
   this passion will have passed.

But he swore he'd never leave her,
   he swore eternal love
by everything that's holy—save
   that emptiness above.

He woke to ice and powdered egg,
   he woke to mud and spam.
His captain said: 'Your caffeine pill.
   We brief at 4 a.m.

Your target will be Schweinfurt, men,
   Herr Hitler's steel plant calls.
A daylight raid—' The gunner said:
   We'll get him by the balls.

'And now I'll let the padre speak . . .'
   The gunner smells the dust
and smiles: *That pin-up on our nose*
   is where I place my trust.
And kiss all four good engines—
   it's ball-bearings or bust!

It's farewell nights in Bedford
 and be seeing you in clover.
It's *auf wiedersehen* Kimbolton Church
 and spot the cliffs of Dover.

Leather, sheepskin, chute, mae west,
 have left the spirit bare
on a climb to 30,000 feet
 through the frozen neutral air.

There's silence over the intercom,
 the radio's one roar,
and ten young men alone in the sky
 beside 3,000 more.

There's clear blue on the Belgian coast
 but blackness deep inland.
The storm in these bolted bomb-bays
 is Thor's own war-time brand.

It throbs its operatic props
 behind a scrim of steel.
A small boy stares up through the clouds
 to watch the news unreel:

then turns back to reality
 and crouches in the dirt
to win that *Kugellager* from
 his brother brownshirt.

The gunner's turret twists and streams
 as fire erupts below,
cathedrals raise a stubborn neck
 to the bombers' lava flow.

But on beyond where Rhine meets Main,
 they hug their thunderbolts,
the gunner in his dream-ball dancing
 last night's fairy waltz . . .

The mild and bitter, jokes and lies,
    the tricks he used to win her,
as if he'd never had a wife
    in German Pennsylvania.

The gunner's mask is itching—round him
    swabs of flak begin:
If only I'd had time to shave . . .
    The flak just nicks his chin.

And now the puffs come close enough
    to pebble the plexiglass.
A portside flash, no crash, but there
    a face and limbs fly past.

But where has the formation gone?
    And what is that shadow doing
slanting below their line of flight?
    That voice—'Hell, guys! We're goin'!'

The bombs drop down. The smoke comes up.
    But somewhere in between
the gunner notices just too late
    one lost B-17.

The Messerschmitts are on your tail.
    Their tracers dart and dare—
the debris of great fortresses
    is falling from the air.

O you've lost your two waist gunners,
    the cockpit is blood and bone,
your ailerons are all shot up,
    gunner, you're on your own.

The bearings'll not get through now,
    the great iron wheel won't turn—
but you are caught in a blazing fort
    and the engines watch you burn.

A telegram ticks through the gunner's nerves
    and worms out of his head.
It says *I regret to inform you*
    and it smells of his unmade bed.

She will not be taking him back with a kiss
    and a Pennsylvania smile.
He will not be sitting to reminisce
    with a Pennsylvania child.

Below him the rock of Lorelei
    reaches to break his dive.
The gunner remembers his mae west and chute,
    for many escape alive,
for many returned to Kimbolton
    to fly their twenty-five.

The gunner lay on the Lorelei
    face down in the cold:
her song blocked out the sun—*Kommst nimmer
    mehr aus diesem Wald.*

To a Blitz Survivor

Pulled out from under the rubble of stories,
mother of pearl, ivory, gut and plaster,
where a stairway uncoils, hissing, and a door
is opening on to the Blackout: a cast,
a props list, suburban dramatics, crammed
into a sealed chimney's priest-hole in your post-
holocaust living room. The doodlebugs hum
down in the skirting. What is it you most

remember about the Blitz? That split-
silence before a V2? Or were they for you
'the best years of your life'? Beethoven's Fate
hammering at the felt, and passing through
into a dusty morning-after, all memory
cleared, the East End like a pub piano
with missing keys, but in the National Gallery
Hess plays on? It's only today we view,

engraved beneath the kitchen table where you slept,
those nights the sky fell in; or overturn
the mask you would not wear; or hear a dropped
chance remark, myths unexploded that were
nothing at the time. Stuka and Incendiary,
your dome has survived. You did not burn,
but married, trying to forget how you had spent
six years in labour, for us to be born.

Otto Hahn in Huntingdonshire

Six miles a day he walked, around and around
that walled garden, fifty times, and for each
rotation a cipher chalked on the wall.

But even after he had left, the number
of scratches on its pale skin would be tiny
compared with the children's shadows etched

into that other ground. He had always sworn
if Hitler cracked the secret of the A-bomb,
he would kill himself. And now this officer

approaches with the news that the Nobel Prize
research into bombardment of uranium
he led has led tonight to Hiroshima.

Nine physicists are amused at such blatant
propaganda, but Hahn stops walking, his face
black, his mind on its one track, flowering

maths, deaths, *Metamorphosen*, as he gouges
his initials, O H, again and again
in the warm August brickwork of Farm Hall.

The angelic voice in the British uniform
is asking why he's so upset—*after all,
better a few thousand Japs than one single . . .*

Hahn's O splits open before his eyes,
a cock's egg that he fantasised has hatched,
Godmanchester cracks, and the Ouse comes slithering.

Two Huntingdonshire Nocturnes

Then there was the night Katie stood out on the lawn,
and watched the Leonids—twenty-seven, I think, she saw
shooting across her vision. We fumble with contact lenses,

the world shifts through our bifocals, but she has seen
stars falling out of her childhood. And now she must learn
at school about the First World War. Her great-grandfather

on the Somme, watching the Very Lights, at that end
of this woodbine century. Tonight she has to pick out the fixed
points on a timeline: pin-pricks like Kitchener, the Kaiser.

.

Fireworks this village is famous for. They come for miles to witness
the Reverend's all-star variety performance, where the judge
once lived who sentenced Guy Fawkes to death.

Catholicism broods here, like the one that wouldn't go off, lurking
in its priest-hole, its side-alley churches. Even our spire flares
a Roman Candle to guide us, as it guided the B-17s

back from their attacks on V2 launch sites, or bombing
a ball-bearing factory. Remember the war. The blackout.
The bagatelle-board rumble from Warren Hill. And then the formations . . .

I met the heir to the fireworks empire at the post-office counter.
He's in the Territorials. Expecting to be called up
to Kosovo quite soon. Bomb disposal. Once November

and the millennium are safely over, he'll be out there, clearing
mines and reminding us that war can never be cleared, however
we celebrate our VEs and our VJs with elaborate triumphant displays,

keeping his eyes on the ground, on the patterns the soil makes.

To August Stramm, Georg Trakl, Ernst Stadler, Georg Heym

'In der Dämmrung steht er, groß und unbekannt'
      Heym

No chair in this no-frills hostel
designed for parties of schoolchildren
studying the war. Four pallets
on two bunk beds, metal,
functional. Bedbugs? Perhaps.

I had wondered, as we swiped
our plastic on the steel door
to get to sleep, what's underneath?
Now I have some idea, for this
is the German cemetery. A wreath,

massive, bronze, discoloured,
like a sea monster scalily
curled in on itself. Graves are
dark slabs, the memorials
monolithic; there is concrete.

Over forty thousand in this
square of earth, taped
as if for a crime scene. Names
wait in strict formation, stand
to attention: *have we reached*

yet nineteen thirty-three?
Against the budding trees
and gathering clouds
are silhouetted four
huge, dumbstruck shapes.

Langemark

Though we tend to think of First World War poetry in terms of the major English figures (such as Owen, Sassoon, Gurney, Rosenberg, and Blunden), Germany and Austria produced their fair share of war poets. Greening's poem meditates on the German war cemetery at Langemark, in West Flanders, a key location in the Second Battle of Ypres. Heym, Trakl, Stadler, and Stramm were important figures in early German Expressionism; Stadler and Stramm were killed in action. KG

To John McCrae

In Flanders fields the poppies blow
Between the crosses, row on row,
  That mark our place; and in the sky
  The larks, still bravely singing, fly
Scarce heard amid the guns below.

We stop at Flanders Fields
and Owen's Coaches
draw up in the same layby.
Watery sun. A farmhouse
opposite has gone nowhere
since pneumonia blew you
away from this hole in
the canal side and it was
nineteen-eighteen. A factory
smoking silently through bare
pollarded poplars on the
far bank. Here, your poem.
There, parked tankers. The coach
driver is pacing, tie over
beer belly. No larks,
just the passing of traffic.
And no chance of a poppy
that isn't paper or plastic.
The children among the graves
are dressed as if they were
themselves a floral tribute.

'Essex Farm', Yser Canal

To Rupert Brooke

This picture shows you
on a stretcher at Port Said,
no longer the golden boy in
the golden room, no honey,
but heat and a mythology
grown molten. April,
and your blood poisoned.
First of the poets, you were
'a stream flowing entirely
to one end' and the one
we reach for still, your
'The Soldier'. Even Blair,
despite Iraq. We like
the thought of that field
within our power. So there
you lie, about to die
but not until St George's,
when they'll bury you
on Skyros, Achilles' home,
and watch the trickle begin
(from brook to river to flood)
out of this dry island.

Grantchester

The Lost Boys

It's 1916. First day of the Somme.
You're out for stand-to, staring into smoke.
Behind you is a field that runs back home.

In front of you are shell-holes, craters. *Come!*
The piper pipes you; there's his magic cloak.
It's 1916. First day of the Somme.

They walked you here (all roads lead to Bapaume)
through mazes, puzzles, Lewis Carroll jokes
(behind you is a field that runs back home)

and left you with some bones, a hat, a drum,
to dream with fairy lights and brownie folk.
It's 1916. First day of the Somme.

The story's ending. Nurse begins to hum.
She'll tuck you up; now there's a sheet to stroke.
Behind you is a field that runs back home.

And soon you'll reach the point where you fall dumb
and happy ever after. Soon, with luck.
It's 1916. First day of the Somme.
Behind you is a field that runs back home.

Tuba Mirum

The long horn of the fjord and what god
up in the highlands summoning Götterdämmerung.

The trumpeting cloud of the first atomic bomb
announcing an end to the war to end war to end war.

The harmonica playing in the small hours, fanfares
of a lost empire, the sun not rising.

The call in imagination, which brings all peace
and freedom avalanching down on top of us.

from Iceland Requiem

Dies Irae

After 9/11

the world collapses with unbelievable speed
to where belief begins again
      the rag and bone
is on the television every night, crying
old iron, old iron
      and terror
makes itself comfortable in our homes

from Iceland Requiem

Coming Soon

remastered from the Old Norse

Alone in my humming suite, the ancient
impresario himself came gazing at me.
What are you after? What are you up to?
I know it all, Odin, even where your eye is.

Deep in Mimir's pool, his pool
of many screens, from which, from your blindness,
each morning he drinks your health, this Head
of Intelligence. Then what? Shall I go on?

All the hardware and software you offered me
as payment for my twenty-four hour news,
my propaganda and public service . . .
I see beyond this narrow orbit.

I see Valkyries auditioning on all sides
for their part in the great epic of the gods.
Skuld has a contract, so has Skögul.
Gunnur, Hildur, Göndul and Geirskögul—
these are the starlets who appear with Odin
on the wide silver world-screen, Valkyries.

The Fate of Baldr or *The Bleeding God*
are the working titles. This feature of Odin's
begins with a close-up of that spindly beauty,
full-grown, top billing, the mistletoe.

From that one opening shot was shaped
a blockbuster of a disaster movie
directed by Hoðr, though even as he did so
the sequel was entering post-production

(in which the newborn Odin android
vows he will track down Baldr's murderer
to the soundtrack of his mother weeping, weeping
for Valhalla).
            Then what? Shall I go on?

A long-shot of someone slumped in the badlands
(subtitle: *Cauldron*), a trouble-maker, looking
remarkably like . . . The camera pulls back
to show Loki and Loki's wife, not happy.
            Then what? Shall I go on?

Dissolve: from the east through toxic valleys
Slith meanders between the arms dumps.
Slow pan across the northern landscape
of Niðavöllum Plain to a hall of gold
for the Sino hordes, then one—a brimming
beer hall—for Brimir the Terrible.

Now cut to a bunker beyond the sun's reach,
on the shores of the dead. Its entrance looks north.
Radiation seeps through its airvent.
Its roof is a chain reaction of snakebones.

There in a montage are the thousand extras—
perjurers, murderers, seducers of wives.
The Daily Niðhogg guzzles on the corpses.
And the Nightly Wolf crunches their bones.

An old bitch sits in the east, in Ironwood,
where she's raised the litter of creatures from whom
will come the one who will tear down the moon,
the one who will home in on you like a warhead.

Already it gorges on internal organs,
spatters the heavens with plasma and lights.
The sun is black for summers unimaginable:
a nuclear winter.
            Then what? Shall I go on?

Sitting in a bomb-shelter, twangling his banjo,
the giants' janitor, cheerful Eggþér.
Above him, from Mutant Wood, the crowing
of Fjalar, the red punk cockerel.

Higher than the gods, castrato Gullinkambi
arias armies awake in their barracks.
Another—skulking in the earth—croons
the colour of hopelessness from Hel's halls.

Garm howls his feedback at the opening
to the final scene, in Gnipahelli—but he'll
be cut. The title will be *Ragnarok*.
The posters will slogan and blare its triumph:

Brother murders brother. Sister sister.
The world gone wild. A plague of promiscuity.
Gun-time. Bomb-time. There's nowhere to hide.
Wind-hour. Wolf-hour. The world spun mad.
Mercy? Mercy is only for innocents.

Children go on playing, but the clear
call of the siren has tripped the countdown.
Heimdall blasts heaven with megawatts.
Odin consults his Head of Intelligence.

The world-web shivers, the system
hacked and trembling, the lone anarchist
breaks loose and the viruses spread.
How are the fatcats? How are the mice?

The radio masts are trembling, the gods
are talking, trapped workmen wail
in the lift they repaired.
                    Then what? Shall I go on?

Garm howls his feedback at the opening
to the final scene, in Gnipahelli—but he'll
be cut. The title will be *Ragnarok*.
The posters will slogan and blare its triumph.

Computer animation: Hrymur in his tank
against Jörmungandur. Sinuous snake-
battle, smashing backs of breakers.
Kamikaze eagle targeting corpses,
shrieking delight as Naglfar is freed.

Muspell's fleet sweeps from the east
Loki piloting marine commandos
from giantland, trailing giant hunger.

Surt whisks from the south, his chopper
chopping the treetops, his rotors
like beams from the sun of battlegods.
Peaks shudder. Camp-women scatter.
The dead throng the path from Hel
and heaven (this could be real) crumbles.

Hlin is hit by his worst luck
as Odin enters to fight with the wolf
and (split-screen) Freyr meets Surt.
Music: *A Lament for the Lost Friend.*

Garm howls his feedback at the opening
to the final scene, in Gnipahelli—but he'll
be cut. The title will be *Ragnarok.*
The posters will slogan and blare its triumph.

And introducing Viðar (Odin dynasty)
who takes out Valdr in a brief scene's
vengeance for how his father has been treated:
with a single bullet.

The world-serpent is unravelling from its hard drive
and rising up as high as heaven's gates.
It's time for Thor. He hammerblows
at the beast in fury, hacks his way into
this macrocircuited earth-locker.

The sun turns black. The land runs to sea.
The bright stars shrink from the sky.
Geysers cannon at fire's wild
pro-life demonstration, scorching the gods.

Garm howls his feedback at the opening
to the final scene, in Gnipahelli—but he'll
be cut. The title will be *Ragnarok*.
The posters will slogan and blare its triumph.

Filter: the earth green once more,
rising for a second time from the ocean,
the waterfalls tumbling, an eagle crossing
the hills, hunting fish. (Strings)

The gods meet again at Iðavelli,
discuss the world situation and consider
the Great Thoughts and Teachings of Odin.

The film ends as we see in the long grass
the wonderful chess pieces, carved of gold,
the ones they had used. Slow motion. Sepia.

Crops growing without being planted.
Wickedness vanishing. Baldr returning
to re-enter with Hoðr and the others the gates
of Valhalla, the heavenly gods' home.
            (Final leitmotif and credits)

        Then what? Shall I go on?

In small frame, Hoenir takes out
(light relief) the divining rods
and the sons of Baldr and Hoðr are seen
relaxing in their ranch: *WINDY REALMS* ...

        Then what? Shall I go on?

Soft focus: a hall rising
brighter than the sun, gold roofed.
It's Gimle Home. There they'll be cared for
the rest of their lives, those who gave
their lives for us.
        Fade.
                Lights up.

Now the dragon comes, dark, glittering,
swooping low from the rear stalls
carrying as he flies towards the screen
the bodies of the dead. It is Niðhogg.

I must go down.

Völuspá ('the Song of the Sibyl') is one of the most important Poetic Edda and a primary source for much Icelandic mythology. This free (and abridged) adaptation of the thirteenth-century prophetic poem was composed at the end of August 2001, after I had returned from visiting my father's wartime base in Akureyri. JG

Eurozone

Incident at Thingvellir

It's all too much for him, this quiet, Black
Ohio tourist, film-wrapped, in his eighties
at least: the lava's caught him; with a crack
his wide-angle has gone. He blurs and teeters

on the ridge, petrified, like tephra thrown
from a far distant eruption to land
cold in this wilderness. He is alone
above tectonics, left without a lens

where two of the Atlantic's moving plates
engage in fierce trench warfare. As I catch
his fingers, grasp them, I feel Europe meet
America across a chasm, edging

him back home. But the miracles of earth
lie unrecorded; that route down to the Rock
of Law through Everyman's Chasm and the birth
of free speech . . . Light's got in, and he won't talk.

*Thingvellir is the site of Iceland's ancient Parliament, the Althing, and a place of geological
importance, where two tectonic plates meet. JG*

Building the Boat

From holt and weald they drag
extinct pines to be our keel,
while someone chips a flint.

From the New Forest they roll
oaks to be carved to inflected
Norman ribs, while someone

is melting copper with tin.
The Greeks give us olive pegs.
The Roman inspectorate moves in

to mark our water-line. And all
is caulked with the beeswax
from a dissolved distant priory.

On the prow is a plaque of laurel
with our dates and a painted eye
in green acrylic. Safely below

and rigged in Egyptian white linen,
a California Big Tree someone
has forged a way of holding in irons.

But our oars are of Norse ash: heave now
towards the Black Sea whose huge waves
rear, long over and not yet.

Borders

We cross borders, and don't even get out
our passports now, as if these mapped frontiers
were a well-healed scar: after all, it's years
since there was anything to fight about
in Europe—brownshirts, the uniformed lout
who looked you in the eye until your tears
ran cold, these are gone; here, no one disappears
except to snatch a wurst and sauerkraut
in the autobahn café. Yet if you've read
or heard tales, or seen newsreels of the war,
you will want to know the faces of those who
crossed this line before you and are dead,
who were startled by an early knock at the door,
or picked out from some shuffling exit queue.

Summer 1986

Autumn Manoeuvres

Ingeborg Bachmann: 'Herbstmanöver'

That's all in the past, is what I don't say.
We are lying again, wallets full of summer's
worthless notes, on chaff of derision, enduring
time's autumn manoeuvres. And no flight path
south with the birds is of any use to us. We are
overtaken by fishing smacks, gondolas, and sometimes
a chip off a dream-heavy marble gets in (through
its beauty, where I am most vulnerable) my eye.

I am always reading in the papers about the cold
and what will come of it, about crackpots, corpses,
about market forces, murders, and of a myriad
ice floes—but find little there to amuse me.
Why is that? I slam the door in the face
of a beggar who comes at lunchtime, because
it's peacetime and one may spare oneself the sight—
though not of the leaves, their joyless death by water.

Let us go on a tour. Let us sit under
cypresses or under palms or in orange groves
and watch at specially reduced prices
sunsets whose like has never been witnessed. Let us
forget those unanswered letters to the past.
Time can work miracles. Though with debt battering
it comes at a bad time. We're not at home. In my heart's
basement, unable to sleep, I find myself again
on chaff of derision, enduring time's autumn manoeuvres.

Castanea Sativa

As if we were trying to   unscrew and open the earth
we torque to ourselves across   Europe, south questioning north
about yield, about harvest   lamenting the vanished hearth
missing the hiss and the spit   comparing fullness of girth

We are proud of our vision   our broad volcano-edge scope
impatient of narrow views   such as those now growing up
in the soft new plantations   that dull inward-looking group
who will not let even one   beam lead a human to hope

And the question unasked is   the oldest of chestnuts still
whether we need other trees   if we're better off single
admired in a rich man's park   Who needs your hot foreign hill
when we're dubbed Spanish Chestnut   granted a wide lawn to fill

and permitted to flourish   *a first class specimen too*
not kept to be felled for our   timber that Normandy knew
was the finest in Europe   though coppices where we grew
palings and hop-poles and beams   still survive here, the last few

No, we're torn, for our roots   go on burrowing no less
keenly than when we arrived   as colonists, Claudius
hankering still for that good   old dependency on us
in feasting and vomiting   all that we've had to erase

Spiked helmets lying in heaps   and rust from a thousand spears
though we relish those seasons   we veteran warriors
in the midst of these copses   away from the sound of wars
left by the British to rot   who prefer to play conkers

Matala

In nineteen eighty-one, reading
Cavafy perhaps, or imagining
tea on Pompey's Pillar,
we were in Alexandria,
a day on its wide strand.

Looking across to when
we sat with friends and someone
related to Laurence Binyon
I think how much has fallen
in Egypt and Libya since we

made that crossing through
violent seas, a childless
couple, whose children now
freely jump the waves
from Africa that break here.

On either side of the bay
we are being watched:
caves once inhabited
by hippies are now like
eye-sockets, families of them.

Spanish Dancer

Rilke: 'Spanische Tänzerin'

As a pale strip of wood and phosphorus
will send out sparky tongues before the head
flares up at your fingers, so these close watchers
see it flickering near, her dance, where it catches
hot, bright, quick in their circle and has spread.

And suddenly it's flame, simple as that.

One look and it's her hair she's set alight
then impulsively twists her entire dress
into this furious pyre with bold finesse,
from which her naked arms stretch out like snakes
alarmed and rattling at each move she makes.

And then, as if she has outgrown the fire,
she takes and hurls the live thing to the floor
haughtily, with imperial disdain
looking down at it, an impotent skin
of flaring rage that offers no concession.
In triumph, sure of herself, and with a sweet
smile on her face she moves into position,
and stamps it out with small unerring feet.

A Letter to My Daughter in Spain

for Katie

The crowd. The cheers. An unsettling pageant.
The plane's veronica—and now with a twirl
of a Cape, you're in Alicante. Touching
to imagine you out there, saying *Cool!*
as you open and bow towards your first
Mediterranean day. You who denied
Spain could prove so very unlike St Neots,
however pluckily my Albéniz kept
insisting as you and your mother fought.

Two daughters of old Taurus I live with
in this tiny arena, where I play the *March
of the Toreador*, slam the door, and bellow
'I'll take up fishing . . .' In fact, I took a tour
for Pisceans: while you, Louise and Clare
faced octopus or squid last night, I was
chased in a dream through this great Dome towards
an open air recital: the *Winterreise*
of J.C. Bach! Which will mean nothing. Although

I've heard you play a piece by him before.
But luck would have the *Blessed Spirits* still
on their black skeletal stand, your silver head
joint resting unmoved by this eldorado.
It's Sunday. And now you're in the market
for fish jokes or squeezing fresh expressions
from Valencia. I'll play *España* or *Don Quixote*
and tilt across Kimbolton Park to Oliver's,
buy eight large oranges to make a fool.

You'll play the castanets of twin best friends
and spin your week down three times thirteen years,
while I repair this bike, turn Rocinante
over and wrench the chain free where it's jammed,
and curse work, oily Protestant wheel that must
keep turning: these are our days, are *my* days . . .
And yours will be a rose between your lips,
a tongue's trill or one hand clapping, perhaps
the need to stamp feet, but no inquisition.

Rosie on the Road to Prague

It's minus one here
and minus much more
in Wenceslas Square
where snow lies deep
and even the drip
of her texts in our sleep
makes an icicle.
The piteous call
of St Nicholas' bell
across the frontiers
is nowhere so fierce
or lovely as hers.

Atelier de Cézanne

Approaching the studio, you must
imagine Lauves as it was before
the black clock acquired hands,
when you could still see the mountain,
when the road was laid with a knife.

.

What isn't up here is down
at the market—the fruit
of the Saison Morte
that lasts a day or two,
transfigured by a squeeze.

.

A plaster cupid: ten times
he painted it, but still could not
capture whatever was battering
its powder wings at the great
panes of his atelier window.

.

The cards that have been dealt
are blank, not even a health warning.
Whatever it is they are betting on
in Kansas, Mannheim, Hiroshima,
this clay pipe knows.

.

The green jug he painted
only once: an aquarelle
in the Louvre, preserving for himself
the original pitcher, its water-
colour, apple of earth.

.

I leave those coats and berets
like the rosary with its narrative
of sister and nun and beliefs
that will never unthread, hanging
in one corner of his room.

.

I take with me that easel,
its sliding windows. Nothing
to be seen but what photography
excludes, the darknesses
of desire and death.

.

*How beautiful it is to paint
a skull*, he said, enjoying
the shadows and a gaze
incapable of offering any
criticism, open-minded.

Roman Fountain

Rilke: 'Römische Fontane'

Two basins, one of them over the other,
rising from an ancient marble round,
and out of the top one water lets itself feather
to water, which underneath it holds out a hand

to receive the gentle conversation in silence
and secretly, showing it only how the sky
behind the darkness and greenness is unbalanced
to something unfamiliar, spreading sly

messages of peace within the lovely shell
without any longing for home, ring after ring,
now perhaps dreamily, just dripping dripping

itself down each of the moss-edged divisions
and on to the final mirror, as if to bring
a smile to the font below at all these conversions.

Borghese

Villa d'Este

More water, extravagant
upshootings and downpourings
of it, unbottled from the
veins of a Borgia. Such force
and power—though to what end

other than to cool the minds
of those overheating here
in the future? Let it rush
and hiss and chuckle and spray
its optimistic excess

down the terraces of five
centuries. Though even Liszt
baulks at so many manuals
below the organ fountain
and though guides simply give up

let it go on running down
from Tivoli into our
trivial hollow ways and
leaden pipework. Just watch us
hold our phones out for the stuff.

After Salzburg

on the night train

Smoke drifts across
darkened snow.
I think of that book
burning memorial
in the square.

From our deluxe
box of folding
planks, clipped
nets, we follow
a scent, skirting

the Alps, going back
on ourselves towards
Cologne. The sun
discovers the Rhine
gold, picks it out.

Verdun

Needles have put these battle-wounded hills
into a deep sleep: innumerable shots
of darkness have calmed the nightmares that wailed
through this landscape by day. Conifer roots
do not need topsoil, will conceal flesh and bones,
and grow so quickly their branches can catch a phrase
from music hall and conceal it until it keens
like a low wind. Conifers can erase
almost everything—warm limbs or cold steel,
craters, corpses, barbed wire, a rusted machine-
gun, a head, a heart, an unexploded shell—
almost everything, to a profound green,
while the fruits that have kept these comatose hills
alive, drop in handfuls like sleeping pills.

Kilmainham

'Kil' means 'church', it means
Divine Providence has decreed
a million Irish should die

and another million must leave
and God knows how many others
beg to be admitted into

Kilmainham Gaol where there is
food at least. He would not
have wanted the rescue of such

or He would have granted them
fishing rights, or planted
charity in the rich souls

of Englishmen. The harvests
revolve and the Birmingham
grandfather clock in the

Upper House clicks on
while Connolly's strapped
into the true meaning

and others learn it by heart:
as the blank bullet papers
on their chests are spoiled

(but not with a cross or a verse)
and the sixteen shots ring out
to Westminster chimes.

To Ireland

for Steve Pollard

In one ear, flute and fiddle and concertina
are crossing to Holyhead on a warm front.

In the other, a viola black with rosin
on frayed gut plays the *Lachrymae* of Britten.

Between: our age's tinnitus, muzak
riffling its one-way pack. Poker-faced, I

mask all but a higher strain, cross-strung
on anticipation of the last trump.

.

Catherine's haunt we leave, and Cromwell's
command, leave Popham's curse on Popery

as he hangs Guy Fawkes: now we burn the miles
across Naseby Field and into the Black Country,

quicken our route to where original green
survives and famine is drowned in the swelling

matrilineal ceilidh—the birth of a one
party state, whose single currency is myth.

.

No snakes, no nightingales, and people
in the west who have never seen a tree.

The rules of engagement in a long siege
are clear: once the wall has come down,

no quarter, no words: women and their young
to be shovelled into a church, the flames

like tongues of roasting songbirds, the screams
like skins being sloughed in darkling timbers.

A new city, made of words. The quatrains
crowd the pavements, phrases linger

beneath the statue of O'Connell, an image
storms the post-office, and evening is full

of poetry readings. How is it Penelope
has kept weaving so long in the wake

of Ulysses? Suitor now reads Tourist
in a re-Joycean denouement. Takes a bow.

The curse of Cromwell is the knowledge
that we are on this side. The Great Hunger

is with us even after a Full Irish Breakfast,
even after we have driven out in search

of ogham to devour, holy stones and fabulous
tales to swallow. Names are unpalatable,

are old iron rations. Drogheda's pill
still makes us leery, say, of Dun-lay-og-hair.

It is like remembering your dreams—
she remains in the snug of consciousness,

fingering primal cerebellum, weaving
labyrinthine fantasies out of the Book of Kells

that translate into unreprievable sentences
or a never-ending melody of defiant

gaiety at top volume on the penny whistle
in an Irish music pub down by the Liffey.

But it is also like a damp squat tower—
Joyce's Martello or Thoor Ballylee.

It is that parody of Maud Gonne waddling
past the Writers Museum. It is that beggar

whose eyes we threw back, the boy fiddling
a jig for all he was worth, which was

an empty cap. It is that couple last night
ejected from the hostel cursing Catholic and Jew.

.

At the Meeting of the Waters, Moore
is less than the children's desire

to go to Ballykissangel, where English
pour in and pout at a soap bubble from

their bright vale, their purest crystal screen. Time
is paused on the tachograph, but the hills

go on being eroded, as young and old
burst for a first glimpse of what they have watched.

.

A car park that closes at 5 p.m. and
a round tower that's pointing to the sixth

century above an unmoved monastery arch.
We march with the rest towards whatever

looks in need of a photograph—some beauty
to rinse our suburban gutters. Here it was

St. Kevin came to find his soul's centre,
says the information centre to itself.

.

No quicker way to lose one's soul than
to be in the company of teenagers on

their first Irish Sunday. They swarm
like those bees, Steve, you told me of,

that turned on their keeper when he stumbled.
He swears, then remembers the healing power

of honey. If only I'd some wax to seal
out that banshee down in the f-loud glade.

.

A U-shaped valley spreads its sweetness
for us, three hunters caught in the hungry ice

after a day at the snout's grubby melt
of rock and cool. As our middle years puff

past the perfect replica of a round tower
and a monastery in the Lower Lake, and reach

the Upper Lake, a shag wings vulgarly by
towards the view we're just too late to catch.

.

Ireland, Ireland, are you all smoky bars
and subterranean shades who let us through

without a ticket, at the cunning word Finbar?
Are you all empty barrows? All shells of Molly

and a Goldsmith in bronze? Respectable respect
for the risen word? A credulous reeling-in

of the legendary? This leprechaun you sold me
replies 'When Irish eyes . . .' if you press its head.

.

The gulls pipe of home, of an inland lake,
man-made, to which I am being wound

by a ruthless absence. Their every raised demand
is an Irish saying, or a fragment of a lost

illumination to a monkish codex
about the exhilaration of the air. *Beware!*

they say. Only gulls believe they can share in
life on the edge of reason, these wild skerries.

.

I walked out to Sam Beckett's anemometer,
away from the Nibelungen dry-docked anvils

of Dun Laoghaire harbour. There was a warning
about the wake from tourist ferries that might

wash you clean off Rennie's wall, and one
about dogshit. But it was that gauge playing

like a bodhrán at Bayreuth, and Krapp
hammered against the wall with Nobel's power.

.

The summoning bell for Mass. Outside,
mass virtuality—a football game, guitars,

space invasion, baton-twirlers, and a nun
pausing at a kissing-gate into the world's

largest women's marathon. No peace here.
Dun Laoghaire harbour is not Innisfree

but a gill-net set to catch more shoals for
Eire to drink with, play at, pierce and throw back.

Kilmacduagh

to Rosie

The tower leans as it has learnt to lean
over time, the century hand conducting
mass from eleven to twelve and on until
it reaches ten past and apocalypse.

A raven craarks its desolate way towards
one of the uppermost dark pentagons
that cut into the stone pointing, as if
cowled monks were posted there: a thousand years

since one last novice hauled a ladder up
and hurled its rungs into the lough for the sake
of mythology, while the Norsemen raged
and gutted, raped and pillaged, as they do.

We approach with a hefty key acquired
from a nearby bungalow, new, a purring
cub of the Celtic Tiger. Above us,
those keyholes into a charred millennium

become the gaze from some extinct and glazed
night creature brought back as a skin out of
the glacial north to hold its fierce posture
in a billiard room, in Lissadell or Coole.

For Jürgen

My friend from Mainz, home of Gutenberg, has written
asking when we'll come. That familiar pattern
of his hand, so very German; he still loves Britain,

or what he thinks we are. It might well appear
we're trapped in a living chunk of *Aufklärung* here
(though light didn't come until the war's final year).

I told his children there would be unicorns in the park
(*Einhorn* for *Eichhorn*) when they stayed with us, way back.
Vanbrugh facade, Adam gatehouse. Such a stack

of reading since he took me first to that famous press,
or taught me how GDR editions would cost less,
and sorted the word order, the world order, yes

we'll visit soon, old friend, to marvel at each spine
precisely in its place, and compare them with how mine
are heaped and dropped and bent; pour me some Hessen wine.

from Huntingdonshire Codices

Der König in Thule

A song from Goethe's Faust
(set by Schubert)

It was up on the Arctic Circle,
a king who had never strayed
was given a golden tankard
by his partner as she died.

He clung to nothing more closely.
He would drain it to the lees
at every banquet as surely
as the tears would fill his eyes.

And when his own death was nearing
he numbered the cities he ruled
and handed them all to the next king,
but not that tankard of gold.

He sat with his knights around him
at the ceremonial feast
in the ancient hall of his castle
on that lofty northern coast.

Then stood, in drink, to honour
the glow of a life though it fade
and threw the sacred tankard
below to the outgoing tide.

He watched it clinking, drinking
its way to the ocean floor.
His eyelids too began sinking.
No drop would he drink from that hour.

1815

It lunges down at Europe, muzzle
of a lone wolf strayed from Ireland,

straining and slavering marsh breath
through Romney, across Dengeness,

to what it can scent from those shaded
wavy lines in the sand. Its eye

is grey with knowledge of events that will soon
see it closed, the origin of a species

buried under brick and tar, yet blind
to such colour as surrounds its advance

towards extinction. It licks the strata
the keeper provides, tongue of Wealden

clay—papillae in their Kentish hundreds
marching mouthwards—and howls through teeth

that should be white cliffs, but now
are verdigris on a two centuries old

statue of the new Duke, who's hurrying
from Vienna; while boring Mr Smith

sits colouring in for the nation
what he sees as a green outline

and not as a wolf snapping at the Straits
of Dover, wanting to devour France.

*Written for an anthology to mark the bicentenary of William Smith's 1815 geological map of Britain—
the first ever made of an entire country. JG*

European Union

1 *The Netherlands*

A wall is breached, the water levels rise,
subconsciousness begins to flood across
the bulb fields into the glass laboratories
that brought the sun to flower where bedrock was.
It flushes out secrets, unchequers yards
darkening in picture frames, sweeps them clear
of fruit and pheasant, old men playing cards
and all still life. It discovers a fear
of dry land, releases the swelling sail
of arrogant white power. It invades
the crow's-nest attic where a Jewish girl
is still in hiding. Its blitzkrieg persuades
Rotterdam to remember history,
old pasturelands abandoned to the sea.

2 *Belgium*

Old pasturelands abandoned to the sea-
grey forest, whose hush-hush has drowned the cries
from those enmeshed in the mythologies
of war, since Flanders first meant territory
laced with needlepoint wire, knee-deep in dark
chocolate shell-holes, where the private dies
for general psychopathologies
to lie beneath an administrative block.
Before Waterloo, Napoleon was engrossed
in paperwork—a strategy recalled
by modern eurocrats: no clause too petty
to advance, no cause too vital to halt,
whatever the cries, the hush, the exhausted
slow hissing submission of industry.

Slow hissing submission of industry
to the power that white water generates
like poetry that has its source in light's
black heart. In the high neutral territory
sacred to St. Lucia, the committee
of Nobel, deep in its word-bunker, waits
to read the world the news: down endless nights
they slalom-skim a glaze of fantasy.
The paradox of darkness out of sun.
The irony of peace from dynamite.
The sheer chuckle of a literary prize
in Swedish, broached and bottled. One by one,
they gutter out—strange names—the same way that
tsunamis conquer and then colonise.

Tsunamis conquer and then colonise
the dragon-ship burial, the sacred ash,
the bog offering, the ribboned runic maze . . .
A seafaring nation, harbouring a cache
of ancient currency, fears its plunder,
prepares to enact again the mighty clash
of Thor and Utgard Loki (the underhand
behaviour of the Frost Giant King
was paid for—as all Europe knows—in thunder):
the old woman Thor took on at wrestling
was really the World Serpent, the rich horn
he was challenged to drain had one end resting
in the sea . . . They say a wise warrior nurtures
the peace, burying storm-force under beaches.

The peace. Burying storm-force under beaches,
they move through the Christmas market stalls
Unter den Linden, paging their futures,

responding to commandments posters call
from a neatly mortared arcade wall
that thou shalt go on holiday next summer
to Dalmatia . . . Slav workers in the mall
would surely say you should not have to fear
that someone near you might select this year
the carpets you laid last. It's time to change
your spots to different spots. Remember, here
you've always lived in petty princedoms—dangerous
to law-breakers, though down in Bonn
whatever crowns were once displayed have gone.

6   *France*

Whatever crowns were once displayed have gone,
but still they prize hard heads above these hearts
we like to think they're soft on—and those parts
for loving which were sickled, tied like corn
dollies, hung up, flung down, kicked, picked and worn
by heart-roasters, blood-toasters, tossed on a Cart-
esian errand through the uterine art
of romanticism, towards the throne
of modern Europe, carved from common bone
inlaid with pensées on necessity and chance,
studded with vital organs of advance . . .
Card-holding revolutionary donors
to all who simply want now to quit France
on an air tour, their only jewel the sun.

7   *Portugal*

On an air tour, their only jewel the sun,
the well-oiled workers of the clockwork lands
head for a rainless world, unclouded fun
in neutral freedom, on natural white sands
from where the sea is just a video
of mindless rock and roll throughout the season:
no smoke, no sail, no subliminal man-o-
war tradition or imperial lesson

flash-framed. Only flies inspect the leftovers:
the earthquake site, the battleground, the sewage
hot-spots so seductive to their ancestors,
prepared for an enjoyable week's carnage
(though finding little turned yet on the beaches
to carrion), *affaires de cœur* with butchers.

8   *Spain*

To carry on *affaires de cœur* with butchers
approach the bullring called Democracy
passing polite refusal of white churches
towards the cervix of their ecstasy
passing the time-warped stargaze of old watchers
towards the wormhole in their galaxy
is knowledge how a people learn to grieve
is knowledge how a nation may survive
the transformation of an old boys' war
to what each Spanish man and woman craves
communion in a holy mass of gore
and flies and dust, to arise in waves
and cheer more hungrily the matador
circling a calm denial of mass graves

9   *Greece*

Circling a calm denial of mass graves,
the generals dream of their Thermopylae,
the poets of a new myth-history,
the millionaires go dancing on the waves,
the tragic actors chant their speech and die,
the slaves have numbers for the lottery.
It has to be, this effort to restore
what otherwise our very fumes would eat,
these loving touches to young Nike's feet
as if she tried on trainers. But in the roar
of Athens, as at Delphi, there is more
to find than when the old is made to meet

the new in a botched join. Strangers you greet
ask what that pride they boasted of was for.

10   *Italy*

Ask what that pride they boasted of was for
as they attempt to keep the traffic running free,
the fountains playing, the tourist industry
awake—that creature closing in its paw
the wealth of those its rampant hunger tore
to pieces—tesserae of art history,
the Pantheon, Giotto, da Vinci:
it eats the Last Supper and it prowls for more.
Perhaps it was for Petrarch to have climbed
his mountain and slow-panned the crimes that love
had been and would be forced into by fame
and, having seen, to have sat down and rhymed
Laura with a truth that would never move:
these few cold peaks, a lyric verse, a name.

11   *Austria*

These few cold peaks, a lyric verse, a name,
and *Eine Kleine* in the coffee shop.
Vienna boys grow ears of purest grain,
whose music is the one unfattening crop
in this petite state. Slender resources
were forced to folds and whirls and creamy heights
by pressures from within, until psychosis.
And now, from a green couch, the mountain shouts
out Bruckner, the lake ringing Strauss Strauss Strauss,
as Schubert's hidden mill stream fights the freeze
and Mozart avalanches the opera house,
Haydn goes on trimming Christmas trees
like Joseph when the angel first arrives . . .
All dream of warmth and youth kicking dry leaves.

12

All dream of warmth. And youth, kicking dry leaves
in Luxembourg Gardens, forgets the rose
of revolution, the pattern of lost graves.
The clever landlocked European follows
his routine in luxurious goodness
and wishes nothing but that those white rows
of stone should never soften his eyes' hardness.
He only desires words like 'buy' and 'sell'
and any others are unnecessary burdens.
Hence, even monosyllables like 'hell'
are skins to be sloughed off—with 'Jew', with 'war'.
He runs his business empire very well
and knows what he will do. He walks his whore
up to a laurel wreath on a red front door.

13

Up to a laurel wreath on a red front door
the children try their voices. The forest looms
about the house at Järvenpää and hums
Tapiola. The children are unsure
if this is right. What have they come here for?
But from the headland of far distant rooms
a sound like the wild geese's wing-beat booms.
It is the master. Ready with the choir . . .
And do not ask him why there is no Eighth
or why, in thirty years, he has not composed
a tune to equal this. He is not to blame
for how the spirits treat him. It is late
to wish for pearls, those lips have been long closed,
though children know things cannot stay the same.

14   *Ireland*

Though children know things cannot stay the same,
their border-country parents try to keep
whatever's precious to them—keep the blame,
the bigotry, the bombs, maintain the cheap
hypocrisy that's served them well, the deep
commitment to intransigence and a pure
religious sentiment that will endure
as long as wolves still like the look of sheep.
They teach their children to obey the call
of lights there on the peace line—orange, green,
(but never red)—to cheer the truth of lies,
to spray (but never read) the writing on the wall,
yet not think what's beyond, not think how when
a wall is breached, the water levels rise.

15   *United Kingdom*

A wall is breached, the water levels rise,
old pasturelands abandoned to the sea:
slow hissing submission of industry . . .
Tsunamis conquer and then colonise
the peace, burying storm-force under beaches.
Whatever crowns were once displayed have gone
on an air tour, their only jewel the sun
to carry, on a fair-day cure. With butchers,
circling a calm denial of mass graves,
ask what that pride they boasted of was for—
these few cold peaks, a lyric verse, a name?
All dream of warmth and youth, kicking dry leaves
up to a laurel wreath on a red front door,
though children know things cannot stay the same.

                                              1997

Words

Brocen Wurde

*'The manuscript begins with two words . . . which have
stayed with me from the moment I first read them'*
  Seamus Heaney

a causeway   where the Norse raiders
waded through mud   a curlew

half starting up   like a stubborn
outboard motor   a copy of *The Battle*

of Maldon   which you read aloud
to the cold May wind   Northey

admits nothing   as the sounds of Anglo-
Saxon disperse   though the bullocks

advance as we leave   as if we might
offer them a translation   an explanation

of what happens in the end   or know the truth
about how   whatever it is   was broken

Hommage

Heaney, how can we hope to follow you
across the bogland of this foolscap shire—
the poets' Grimpen, the midden of the bards?
Yet who else would we take for guide? Sure-footed
as Wordsworth and with John Clare's blackthorn eye,
iambically testing texture, surface
tension, prodding to gauge the weight and depth
of every step; your steady voice would charm
through fret and whiteout, yet serenely chant
a bullfrog chorus, whistle a Black Dog
away, commune with bog people, with drowned
forgotten poets and the untuned ribs
of stragglers still not quite returned from Troy.

The Source

At the precise centre of the Heath, in the middle of a wily
convoluted labyrinth, a troy town, a mizmaze, whose origins
are lost beyond druidry, at the exact centre, there is said
to be what can only be described as a mouth. Others have called it
bog, marsh, slough. Some have had coarser names for it.
But it's a mouth. It is likely to be the very source of language,
the pit in which all Indo-European snakes seethe.

You poets, it grumbles, you're just producing landfill. And you're each
convinced your work will live for ever. Why do you even bother?
It's about as much use as these marks on this stone I've been sucking
and means sod all to most people. The only poetry
is oral poetry, stand-up, slam. The kind of thing you did
for seven-year-olds when you put on magic shows out here (remember
Fairey?) reciting Ted Hughes to accompany your Floating Zombie.

Where Fairey Aviation vanished into folklore, at Hayes
it may be heard still, the patter, the abracadabra, the gasps.
Wait until fog comes, or Iceland scatters its dust,
then think of it as Grendel's home, as you let yourself be swallowed
crying out to St Catherine, St Anne, to Theseus, to Serapis, to Puck
and follow the staring patterns of the spirals, cup and ring, its mis-
direction of children from Hollywood to Tintagel, from Hilton to Wing.

To Johannes Gutenberg

You taught us how the world could be contained
between stiff boards, reduced to type, to a row
of lead: preserved, passed on by mirror-code
to any future, even this, where multi-laned
our information runs its rings, hare-brained,
and wails and mocks the passing of the slow
cold dawn of print on page. Books will still grow
as grapes are red. But look—this untrained
circuitry is cocooning us: no need
for labour here, the hourly vintage plays
direct from every lap, its icons bubble
a character from light with lightning speed
and disregard for all you hauled, screwed, pressed
out of the dark—yes, and thought immovable.

A Text Message to Anglesey at Pentecost

Hold this net in your hand and catch the winds from Holyhead.
Let the standing stones ring with the words that no one is speaking.
Call back and tell the gulls that it is Dafydd ap Gwilym.
May the lost languages cross the widening straits of our age.

A Letter

Fleet, 29th October 1998

Floods in the west.
Gales possessing our vanes,
our vessels. Then, your name

before Camilla and Charles
Attend Society Wedding:
Ted Hughes is dead. Wild

horses chafe at Chesil Beach
and its hierarchy of pebbles—
Lyme Regis to Portland Prison.

The Fleet is unruffled.
Geese gather there, a million
quills of rhyme empty

and ready to take to the blue
vacancy. It had been
a bright and tranquil day

between storms. We fought
to the brink of separation
past Maiden Castle: *Right!*

you can drop me at the station!
At Dorchester, pax, thinking
of Hardy and of the children,

ourselves again with mummy
amulets, ushabtis, the heads
of Osiris, Anubis, and other

equipment for the afterlife,
our six-year-old Tutankhamun-
struck by the waxworks

at this exhibition, peering
through a crack in the wall
to behold a golden treasury.

Now I stand where a coastguard
kept watch over Tennyson's
and Masefield's tricks, and hear

the wind in the cowl intone
its pibroch, the horizons howl
Prometheus must not be spared,

waves rejoice and again rejoice
that hawk and crow and priest
are grounded—hear all this

remembering on the edge of Dartmoor
that tied farm cottage, moored
to a bank of the Exe

where we existed for a year,
two scientists and I: one night
the river swelled almost up to

my ears. I could hear the beat
of impending black subsidence
in my sleep. It was there

I sat up all night with Crow.
From there I sent you my three
Devon plays, my nature poems,

there I gently lifted up (as if
a salmon would take a fly
though he knew it was hooked

and he would be kept in a net
and put on display, as I have
in writing this) your letter.

Two Sonnets from Hawthornden

DRIVING THROUGH BEECHES

Beyond tall beeches, which are books, whose leaves
turn steadily to October, our cars
are finding reading hard: they slur across bars
of sunlight, skimming on in search of movies.
Though rooks recite the law and sober coveys
may tut their way down those neat rides, out here's
a game of getting there. So don't ask where's
the fire. It's in our heads, the spark that drives
us through this wood we'll never know, its aim
to lay waste distance, not to teach how slow
real progress is. Yet the beeches hold sway,
believing they'll be proof against our flame,
that in another hundred years they'll know
as much as they know now, and ring this day.

MARY SIDNEY

That night no moon could brighten brought a moth
to Spain's fire, but I have preserved Arcadia
in these beds for him. Gardeners keep faith
though others lose it. How many pretty heads
have been planted now? My brother's death
still climbs the years with sad steps. These last threads
of psalmody I sew for him beneath
our lawns, our hedges. Turn on your radio:
there is another life. I sing the Lord's
song in a strange land, where your every breath
will play back notes in consort with new words.
Now find the key and from that treacherous path,
the Lady Walk, look down while fear and doubt
are still in bud, and follow the river out.

Wild Spiders

'We are like a lot of wild
spiders crying together
but without tears'
    Harriet and Robert Lowell

I know the black widow lives
on the east coast of America—
and not out in the backwoods,
but here in the house of the white
common reader. So when

I took down that blue fading
hardback, *Tudor Poetry*,
to discover in it Sir Walter
and Sir Philip, damp, as if still
weeping for the court of Elizabeth,

I willed her, creature of myth,
carrying blood in her hourglass,
to gracefully step from a ruff
of web and stand naked: 'Yes,
look here for my poets! But then

close the book and look about you.
This far our language flew
to renew itself with venom
when America was a sweet pursuit
to distract my buzzing lovers.

But now it is the centre of another
age's spinning. Let your fingers,
like my eight legs, run along
time's shelf until they touch
the bent spines of softbacks,

fat Lives, ghost-written,
dust-covered sex, detritus
of psychology, and one slim
confessional poet . . . The shelf ends.
But there on the far side of the word

processor—where anyone, John,
could write creatively, where you can
let your fingers join as if in prayer,
as if to think. And allow yourself
(O slow, fresh fount!) to cry.'

Passaic Falls, Paterson

The Falls are approached through
an area where it's best to drive
with the car doors locked.

We park near the stadium, crunching
the shed scales of some crowd
that has coiled elsewhere, walk

naturally as we can towards the roar
that the stadium android swallows
nightly, along with these spearhead

palings, this barbed-wire-and-bronze
statue of Alexander Hamilton,
who first thought to tap the Falls . . .

Not even an aerosol names
William Carlos Williams
whose echo sounds in my ears

like a churning mill. Though who
in Paterson has heard of him
or knows Paterson is a poem,

now that the Falls are a hangout
for pushers, hookers, and
kids on the brink? We step

on to the primitive plank bridge
and language fails us.
Feeling like Dr Williams'

tongue depressor, I look
into the gorge and witness
a spectacular infection. Above

the hundred streps, a kid
sniffs lighter fuel. He looks
like that Nubian on the West Bank

of the Nile who held an oil lamp
guiding us down dry desert steps
into the Tombs of the Nobles.

One Could Do Worse

for Rosie

Today you found a handy perch
fifteen feet up our silver birch.
Its branches shrug there, make a Y
you've shaped your limbs round in reply.
That's something Robert Frost, whose boy
climbed on and left his girl to dry
her long pale hair in simile,
did not have the vision to foresee.
We cry: *don't slip, don't fall asleep!*
But you've no plans to swing or leap,
just sit where no one's been before
except the cat, who's down next door
appalled to see you, book in hand,
swaying above our neighbour's land.
You would, you said, have liked to take
the Works of Shakespeare, but they'd break
the branch. Indeed. I'd stick with Frost.
Much safer if you're tempest-tossed.

Bad Fences

So, Frost, what do *bad* fences make? Having just
left one so rattlingly ungainly, a poulter's measure
of a line without craft or gift or design, you'd not trust

for chatting or as a net: a free verse affair, whose slant
posts mark random stresses in my hammering head
from a day of struggle with storms, refusing to say *I can't*.

Good poets make bad fences? It would be consolation.
Where's a critic when you want one to lob back a comment
on our old glass shower door or this new exhibition

of headboards from our first double bed, exposed
to neighbourhood watch, or me unable to do the job,
too proud to call in a man? Would I have been roused

to this pitch of frustration had I not conveniently forgotten
that when we first moved in there were no fences at all,
a right of way ran clear across four gardens?

What now we call the back was then the front: a well,
a copper, coal-house, privy; and tales of the night soil
collector who would trot across and beyond this very pale

I'm lying beside and trying to fix, but failing. *Shit!*
Shit! The answer, Frost, undoubtedly is: bad fences
make bad tempers. I'll try the internet.

from Huntingdonshire Elegies

A Hurt Hawk

They downed a Nighthawk over Kosovo today,
the so-called Stealth; its non-reflective span
twitched the finger on a Serbian trigger.

I think of Jeffers out at Carmel Point
shooting his red-tailed hawk and feeling
on balance he would have preferred to kill a man:

Jeffers, who was far from locked in those barbed
allegiances and poisoned springs of a land
fought over since the fourteenth century,

whose options and whose limits were as clear
as the cliff edge where he hacked out lines
to stack with the stones he cut to build Tor House,

whose vision was a radar that could see into
the night, see through night's mask, but still
mistake a fully loaded bomber for a bird.

Poet's Bestiary

Attempting to hammer some live thing out of the words,
black and white, green, it hangs on the feeder.

.

A sentence better not to have set free, it curls
and plays dead, v on its neck, forked tongue.

.

Carelessly it leaps from home to home, rattling
Grey I may be, but I still have all my teeth.

.

No ideas, but listen, here comes Ottava
Rima, taps on a web-page, sits there waiting.

.

Between a stroke and an attack, she's wrapped
around my arm like a blood pressure monitor.

.

In a brown study, at last words begin.
That ******* white dog squatting on our lawn.

John Donne in Huntingdonshire

In Keyston, the hacked clay waits for a memory stick.
Daffodils hunch like PC objectors to Good Friday's
mowing ritual. I have tried the church door. It's locked

and Alpha Dot Security have left the world their hologram.
I'd hoped to find some memorial to the lover and divine
who held the living here, inside—instead, as I am

texting you and Huntingdonshire's dead give stony
silent rebuff to the A14, reversing lorries,
jets, and one lone collared dove—it's Donne

himself who climbs, ignoring me, not quite believing
he's agreed to this outlandish benefice (the roads
knee-deep from London) to please his wife. A *living*?

His roving years are past and yet that country moll
who wouldn't catch his eye is enough to make him wish
the gargoyles would stop poking tongues; and to recall

another girl, then others, row on row, their features,
lips and breasts, but not their names. The busy lover
would have carved them into these divine grey beeches.

The tower's shadow ticks. He must have felt the arch
conceal its burden as he touched this warm stone, breathing
stained light, then slipped out through the porch.

A bell tolls and down goes that unruly sun.
His wife's expecting their next child; but by next year
John Donne. Ann Donne. Un-done.

Four centuries. For us, it's thirty years; and still
you share a poet's bed and send me words from 'The Ecstasie'.
Keep texting love: that brief vibrating thrill.

from Huntingdonshire Elegies

At Pope's Grotto

A shadow opens the door—
a nun, for whom
there is only one Pope

but who is gentle, kind,
remembers all our names
and though we have made

no appointment—*shut
the door, would you, John*—
she lets us in.

.

The last of just three
left in this convent
to be disposed of soon,

she takes us down waxed
and timeless corridors
holding a key.

My daughter stifles fierce
rage, managing
to be heroically polite

in reply to Sister Mary's
quiet iambics—
What lovely children . . .

.

Gloom: a tunnel, rough
walled, fragments of
fossil, fool's gold.

Stumps where once
the stalactites from Wookey,
holy relics, hung.

Blank, tarnished verso
that was a mirror—
a camera obscura

to record all the sinuous
joys of the River Thames
beyond this pentameter-

length retreat. *Here,*
says Sister Mary, *is St
James and here . . .*

.

Centuries before anyone
thought to hide the public
from smart bombs

it was used to shelter
a hunchback under siege
by his own *Iliad.*

Then as a bunker
from which he could take
poet-shots at pride.

Finally, the laboratory
where his genius could
perfect dunce-warfare.

.

We are squinting down
the muzzle of that
distinguished cannon

shell-gagged beneath
the tides of freedom
and hypocrisy

to see a romantic green
reply, but the gate is
locked, with good reason.

The Sonnet

after Goethe

'It is a sacred duty when creating
to honour old traditions: therefore, you
may join us in this steady marked-out queue
and follow all our movements as you're waiting.
We find such limitations are exciting,
when spirits are too urgent to subdue.
It offers them a way of shining through,
perfected in your polished formal writing.'

I wish I could. That's always been my aim:
to measure feelings, word by metred word.
A sonnet, rhymed—I would be proud of it.
But no, I just can't settle in this frame.
I'm used to carving single blocks of wood,
but here need superglue to make things fit.

Somersby

'root and all, and all in all'

A sonnet? Not out here. Even his wolds
are Kraken and Excalibur, revealing,
sinking back. Note, as you approach, a scowling
face, an outcrop, carved. Legends. Half-reaped fields.
An empty settle. There's a babbling child's
remembered brook. The font. A new-style calling
of kine in with a car horn, their line filing
in search of its epic muse. She'll wait, holds

the six-bar gate, and sings. But, Tennyson—
whose house is just below, beside the grange
and opposite his father's tiny living—
do people love you still? High among crannies
on the crazed green sandstone church tower, strange,
that one perennial, bright yellow, thriving.

Stanzas from the Grande Chartreuse

They set off through the bitter cold, and he
is full of what a night it was—the cells,
the silence, candlelight, and pax—while she
is longing for some warmth. There are no mules
and he's decided they can walk: the mist
has gone, so Matt, of course, cannot resist

the lure of Alpine peaks. His pristine wife
takes some convincing, having spent the night
apart while he inspected man's belief
in what he can't believe. She'd sensed her fate
last night as they approached: the chill, the roar
below from an unseen river, Guiers Mort.

At least this morning he has deigned to speak,
is even cheerful (*Excelsior!*) as they climb
his choice of narrow, slippery mountain track
for three hours, till she asks about the time
and where they are. The high Alps glisten.
He starts to talk, and she can only listen.

By chance, they find a chalet, where he hires
a mule and then insists they carry on
to Les Chapieux. A local guide declares
it isn't wise, but Matthew Arnold's done
with teachers—nature (as Wordsworth said) is school.
So Fanny Lucy climbs on to the mule.

Without a saddle, perched there, she is led—
her poet-husband trailing far behind—
towards a maze of ice (if she had stayed
in Hampton!) along a razor's edge, no ground
in sight, a snowy chasm stretching out
beneath her, epic similes of doubt.

It is as if he's somehow conjured this
from his own mind's cold sophistries, a vent
of bubbling myth. As though Empedocles
were holding that long rein way out in front
and leading her beside a seething cone,
where sparks of warmth mean poetry alone.

Sweet

What? My wife browsing through
her old Anglo-Saxon texts
as I come home from an evening
of hearing parents tell me
how their kids love their Kindle?

Wē cildra biddath thē
thæt thū tæce ūs sprecan rihte

I listen to the scratch and crackle
of eth and thorn as she recites
one of the colloquies.
                            Hwaet wille
yē sprecan?
                    The single flare
of a hedge sparrow spurting through
the mead hall.
                        Hwaet rēce wē
hwaet wē sprecan?
                                The hedge-hopping
stubble-blazing life of the poet
who had never heard of homework.

Fires

There's one made up of the Norse
world and Anglo-Saxon
spear-shafts at the bottom of our garden,
its golden key-bunches seared
to a scarred grey homonym
by morning. Damp. Misty.

I've built another out of
three small logs from the elm
they felled for us in May—
an eighties offer, delivered
through our letterbox with a scattering
of poetry, disease-resistant.

Though not foolproof. Sapporo
Autumn Gold may glow
from the grate all day, but I
am in another room, trying
to make green cuttings catch
with a few breaths and this paper.

Skáldskaparmál

Advice to Visitors

Skáldskapr's igneous
forces can erupt
at any time to destroy
the mosses and flowers

its powers unimaginable
yet its molten out-
pourings will as swiftly
cover a plain

with rubbish and
bleak monotony
as with thrillingly
balanced pillars

where the scalding
springs bubble
mud colours
for our amusement

and geysers perform
without need of soap
their wash cycle
as if nothing could

misbehave, shake
down our comfortable
dreams or hold up
our 4x4 beliefs

to glow like horseshoes.

'Skáldskaparmál' means 'the language of poetry' and is the title of one of the sections of Snorri Sturluson's Edda in which he lays down the rules for would-be skalds. JG

Bragi

Bragi runs a small poetry press.

He publishes the work of the lesser known and little read.
He edits a magazine called *Kvasir's Blood*.

But Bragi finds that people are no longer very interested in poetry
or in seeing life through baleen-ribbed metaphors.

They have other fish to fry.

They have their cars, their videos, their hi-fi.
They feel no need for words wrought into significant patterns,
words that require more than a quick scan
to glean instructions or the outline of a plot,
taut words that quiver against your cavity wall
and sing of the Aesir and the Vanir and the winning of the mead.

And the poets themselves don't know what they should be writing about.

Not war—they have never experienced war.
Not gods—they have lost their belief in gods.
Not love—love has been discredited.

The rotation of themes has reached its fallow season.

On to the worked-out prairies,
Bragi is throwing blood and bones and ash.

In every furrowed brow he will sow new images.

from The New English Edda

Three Poems after Hölderlin

BREVITY

'*Die Kürze*'

'Why so abrupt? Don't you enjoy writing poems
    any more—when what you used to hope in those days,
        in those optimistic days,
            was that you'd never have to stop?'

Poems reflect how things stand. Would you want to romp
        in the pink as the sun goes? It's gone. The ground's cold
        and the tawny owl riffles
            against your eyes, discomfited.

TO THE YOUNG POETS

'*An die Jungen Dichter*'

Fellow poets, it's possible that after much
    teen-wasting duck shot we are at last maturing
        into something more swan-like:
            however, don't stick your neck out.

Stay tuned to higher possibilities, but love
    the everyday—except booze, prose and school-teaching.
        Should you think I'm too severe,
            just step outside and ask Nature.

COURAGE OF THE POET

'Dichtermuth'

Aren't you a part of everything in existence?
   Doesn't Fate have special plans for her protégé?
      So what's to fear in this life
         for any man of woman born?

Whatever happens, it's all good, so why don't you
   simply enjoy it—unless there's anything you're
      holding back, something that might
         cause problems at passport control.

In the same way as a vulnerable swimmer
   tempted by a river or by silvery waves
      or the silent glacial
         call of fjords, still likes to keep

humanity to hand, the living, the laughing,
   for whom we poets—cheerfully ever-trusting—
      take the plunge. How otherwise
         could we touch anything profound?

If waves occasionally claim the most fearless
   in the fury of a success that reached too far,
      smelt too tempting, and the voice
         becomes a blue name on the wall,

they died gratified and on Primrose Hill or off
   a bridge or in Puget Sound, some student's headphones
      catch elegiacs in tides,
         in traffic or in faint hissing.

Another poet passing by the famous spot
   one evening will glance at the plaque and half recall
      the story, thinking, no, not
         like that—moved—and go on their way.

Sylvia Plath

The snow flies in all directions
but doesn't settle, elusive as
reputation. We all need a page
to write our names on—
yours is on Primrose Hill

where Yeats left his chalkmark
and children who have never heard
of either of you long to make
a snowman. It's half term.
Those who were born that day

are announcing their half century
on Facebook, a blue plaque
in the cloud. Your sylvan rides
turn to slush, pavement-grey, until
the next fall. One year in ten

there's such a winter: warm yourself
at the editorial bonfire, watch
the dying art of hedging
and ditching, forgive the crystal
deceptions, and let Ariel go.

11th February 2013

Yeats's Tower

Steps that are hard
to learn: but follow

the master as he sits
watching the dancer

and the dance, music
passing under his window,

and let your feet
attempt the slippery

winding rhyme and
clause and line

break up to the
battlements where you

can see the whole
country, where you

can see the stars
move in patterns

everyone knows
but no one knows

how to follow,
so hard the steps.

Ars Poetica

You have to be a little bit unbalanced to write:
poplars leaning above the Kym that whisks a white
duck or paper cup to the bridge and out of sight.

You have to have something you are holding back
or attempting to suppress, a grief, an anger, a deep dark
resentment or dissatisfaction. The willows crack

as they are meant to do. But they shoot free of the break
in lines of three, and then into buds that will make
catkins and leaves and flowers. You have to be awake

when others are dreaming, and dream when others are out cold.
The waters, muddy, persistent, irresistible, hold
your life beneath the surface and will soon have sold

you down the river if you don't reach out for a reed,
a straw, an overhanging rush, a feather, tread
water and pull yourself up word by word.

from Huntingdonshire Codices

Homage to Tomas Tranströmer

'my poems are meeting places'

My daughter says the landscape today is like somewhere in Sweden.
It's certainly like the interior of a Tranströmer poem,
a dream territory with car headlights through trees and sealed
carriages at a halt, islets, icy bells or piano
notes among pine needles, cones filtering the dark

from a north where I'm having breakfast. The late eighties, and there
he sits with various Eastern Europeans, a Bloodaxe affair.
We don't speak, though he looks up towards a leak
in the ceiling that drips, drips (our host is mortified),
diversion signs, points change, something going on.

It must have been a few months later he had the stroke
that means he can only use his left hand and barely talk.
Haydn listens. The man with the hammer goes on walking
beside the wheels of the train. *Like a dream*, I agree
as we drive, still nothing coming on the other side.

Death of the Poet

Rilke: 'Der Tod des Dichters'

He lay there, head and face propped up, washed out
and in denial, on a kind of pillow shelf:
all knowledge of the world, the world itself,
torn from his senses, dropped back to a gulf
in which the year gives passing little thought.

Those who knew him before the illness struck
had no idea how far he was at one
with all of this: the valleys, meadows, mean-
dering beck, they were the essence of his look,

that look—which was defined by this whole view,
turning as still it does for him to cherish;
his deathmask, yes, it's truly nightmarish,
but vulnerable, delicate, like a fruit
cut open to the air that starts to perish.

After a Poetry Workshop

Today, half looking for a colleague's grave,
a craftsman, a teacher, who was born in this place,

I find a door—that when we first came, the month
we learnt we were to be parents, was locked—

opening on the swell of history, the gulls' cry,
a distant playground shriek. That land is drowned

and Merlin with his staff has crossed to Camelot:
not a single stone that says Pendragon here

among the Chilcotts, Wades, Tremains, though follow
the river up to Slaughterbridge and read

what's written in the water. Storm clouds wipe
the moor black; white arms seem to be swimming

for someone's very survival. And I perch
in drizzle on a name that's worn away

holding *The Parish of Tintagel, Some
Historical Notes*, forgetful of my reasons

and all distance. 'Preparation for death'
I want to say when they ask what poetry is

then find their tongues becoming Cornish slate
and every scratch or squeak an elegy.

Notes

A Question

What is music? A sculpture carved out of air.
A counterpoint of earth, water, fire in the air.

It eats into the barnacled hull of work and pay,
drawing out its gold-fingered wire from the air.

Collar and veil and cocoon of a flame that converts
touchpaper lives to its pyre. It's the air

that the clay on bootsoles wishes for when it urges
our feet more slowly, much higher, where the air

is only fit for spheres. Music is the seed
within such bubble inspirations that aspire on the air,

then burst into canopy. It is a figured fermenting
in our cellars, the progress of Gaia through the air

to demijohn, a greening of black ashbuds, when all
sobriety and sackcloth vows expire to the air.

Syncopations

Unless there was time, there could not be music.
It plays between the beats as the wind
in the telegraph wires. There is no music

on a high, bare island. None on Wyre
or with Muir and his bones in the glue factory.
Only faint horse voices. But follow the wire,

its sharp, infectious whistling, to where days
beat time to the percussion and the silent
brass of Passchendaele, and birds are in a daze

of bark and cortex and centuries of sycamore,
sound-wave rings from a shattered phil-
harmonic. Unless there was time, there'd be no more

victories over chaos, nothing would count, one
two, one two, nothing would march
or waltz again, dance again, there'd be no battles won

for metre and rhythm or the sweet deceit of not
rhyming to a time signature, these are the crewel-
work, the filigree, the knotting and the final knot

possible without which there could not be music
that plays among the high, bare wires as the wind
between the distant poles, where there is no music.

from The Masque of Time

Alive Alive O

We'd stand around the piano
like long shadows cast
by Victoria, like that dark
custom of drawing the curtains
when somebody died. I'd turn
the pages through John Peel
and the Vicar of Bray and find
Sweet Molly Malone—
poignant story of a girl
who wheeled her shellfish
through Dublin's fair city,
commemorated there, off
Grafton Street, the 'tart
with the cart' . . .
                    And we'd sing
our hearts out around
my mother's upright. No video,
no television even, nothing
to distract us from reaching
alive alive o
                    But those
bodies clustered in her
pool of light have been picked
off, have left this landing
stage, swallowed in one
salt gulp by time
and I'm alone now, looking
at the empty wooden o's
where candelabra were removed
to modernise the piano, or listening
how that A always sticks
as she plays, and crying
without a chorus, *cockles*
and mussels to her curtains.

Holst

Marching into prayers at primary school
they used to play a 78 of *Mars*.
There began my love of music
and of astronomy. The perfect fool
had found his round peg's round hole:
to sing squarely of the stars
to a generation who would lose its
sight and hearing before it had grown old.

Record Factory

Near Hayes & Harlington you'll notice the words His Master's Voice
in large black letters, close to the trains (as yours brakes)
and a factory's half-demolished remains. The Heath

has never stopped recording, although we lack the means
to play it back. A wax cylinder recalls a buzz
that was going round long before the mead halls.

How steel wires stiffened. The lac insect hummed
its dance-hall abundance. Reel turned to reel,
and discs unrolled their vinyl over the dead level.

Look where the tracks catch the light in different ways,
according to their character, and the way each has its own
borough-bred voice. What is it called, this nostalgic compilation?

You can cover it in two or three minutes on the Heathrow Express.

                .

Under the new extension to the record factory at Hayes

(the one I used to cycle to at 33 rpm
or 78 if I was late
dealing with returns, unwrapping the layers and layers, weird
enclosures, hieroglyphic complaints, clocking off,
clocking on again, the days of counting the hours
only to place them unceremoniously in a skip so they could be
taken through the sacred gates of EMI
and somewhere in a field to the west
     whose location is yet to be
        established
           quietly buried)

they found a statue
from the second century BC, Egyptian, of a priest
carrying the shrine of a god
as if he had picked out
a boxed set of the complete recordings of every mass
for the dead ever written from Beethoven to Berlioz to Britten.

Now here he is, off to the checkout, waiting, waiting
long after long players, long after the latest Adams
MP3, still waiting to pay

when a small dog nips across to him and says
Drop what you're doing. There's an important message from the Master.

'Record Factory', which comprises portions of poem XXXV in Heath, is constructed of the author's recollections of an early job at EMI Records. The little dog, Nipper, and the slogan 'His Master's Voice', were employed in many advertising campaigns and logos for record labels, including EMI, HMV, and RCA Victor. KG

Strings

Chaconne, a single violin against the world, performed
by Grumiaux the magnificent: our universe tamed
for thirteen minutes, its circus act live-streamed

to this small hut in Huntingdonshire.
I listen, recalling the first fiddle piece I ever
played, on open strings: *A Toye*. This reverie

is enough to send me on my way. You'd think for once
I'd stay awake instead of going to join those clowns
inside my head. Didn't I feel eternity pounce

and gnaw at the bars of time? Now I'm making friends
in my dream with marching gladiators, while Belgian hands
craft their filigree, unheard. Though the music ends

Bach goes on pushing the Age of Reason to the edge
of reason, like a blade in Flag Fen, sacred, such
ingenuity and refinement, yet too deep to reach.

from Huntingdonshire Codices

After the Interval

Such disappointment that the celebrated
Belgian violinist was indisposed,
unable to perform, would be replaced
by no one of note. You knew you were fated
never to hear him play, though you had waited
since 1945. You could have passed
on the second half, but (not to waste
an evening out) you stayed. And now it's started,
the river flowing darkly by the Strand,
that flower-summons, Big Ben's harp-harmonics,
and cymbal rush hour. 'A London Symphony'
you'd never heard before, whose movements send
you back to find your blacked-out heart is on its
way downstream, towards the unrationed sea.

Sweet Vale of Avoca

My daughter is singing
at the Meeting of the Waters.

She is wearing the green
coat I have criticised

for its impractical
embroidery, its dragon

coiled ineffectually
against the cold.

An old fisherman
is standing by his line

like a man who does not
exist as one stream

passes into another
and there is a brief

glittering quarrel
around nothing.

But it is warm here
in the October sun

as her voice rises
in its scales, leaping

from 'bright waters'
to 'the last rays'.

Birtwistle in Jamestown

When Rosie started pressing the buttons on her Pocahontas game
as I was trying to follow *The Triumph of Time*, I threw it
across the room in a rage. And then I remembered the real

Jamestown, founded by Sir Edward Wingfield of the Priory
here in Stonely. A virgin land he entered on, like young
Birtwistle confronting class and music. Patentee, artist

established their colonies, raised defensive palings,
played the crusader, blew fanfares at the tribes who gathered
waving hatchets and whooping. One night at the Proms

I saw Pierre Boulez conduct from the autograph score,
turning its pages like huge leaves of a tobacco plant.
One day at the school I walked into a drama class

and heard the wail of *The Triumph of Time* and called out
to my friend, who was always there . . . Fifteen years ago.
And the Prom must be twenty-five. 'Writing music is like

driving a car at night, you can only see the headlights
and get an idea of the landscape.' Stonely Priory's dissolution
clinging to the hill. The soprano sax singing its lament

in Hatchet Lane. My daughter looks daggers at me.
The procession passes: an elephant, an angel, the grim reaper.
Our American friends ring and ring: there is no answer.

from Huntingdonshire Nocturnes

Middle C

Those piano keys are keys to the doors
you never opened. When in my innocence
I bought you Mussorgsky's *Pictures*, and force-
marched you through The Great Gate, you had the sense
to prefer a Promenade . . . but, of course,
that's you, to walk the self-effacing way.
Remember Middle C? The girl who looks
down for a keyhole to help her, then one day
she's climbing up to 'perform' (your wry laugh!)
and finds that grand pianos don't have locks.
A moral, yes—but Mum, not even with half
a smile quote me that church bill (*THE MIDDLE ROAD—
THE ROAD TO FAILURE*) and say, 'My epitaph'.
You only followed the way the music flowed.

The Rhenish

At the Bridgewater Hall, Manchester, 9th June 2007, with my mother

Schumann threw himself in the Rhine, and now
it rises by capillary action through
the strings and horns, a cathedral sound
no morning-after pattern of the Allies'
mercy could rival. This stinging in the eyes
is Kölnisch Wasser the music draws
out of an old canal in Manchester
where youngsters singing from the pub stagger
across a lock gate. Behind the Bridgewater,
a song-line from the Rhenish Symphony arched
over the barging menace of the dark
still glows and points to where our gold is parked.

Field

Think of those artists who will never
escape the shadow of one they had
the bad luck to precede, who did

it first but not quite as stunningly
as the name we now remember. John
Field, for example, 'inventor of

the Nocturne', who nodded off while
Chopin opened the five-bar gate
and walked all over him.

July 12th

for Evelyn Glennie

Protestantism beats the air polyrhythmical,
crowds press to the barriers at Drumcree.

While here in a middle England chapel, we file
to occupy all sides of a loaded stage.

Bombs home-made from treaties soaked in hatred
burn the Garvaghy Road. We look at an oil drum

or turn a discreet page. The RUC get out
their riot shields, the troops load rubber bullets.

We prepare our applause, a tam-tam waiting
to swell, a secular gamelan. Black hats

attend to the Grand Master of the Orange Order.
We—to a loose gown and hair, bare feet.

Peace is forgotten, all palms are closed to it.
But she picks up two sticks and begins a new

piece called *Darkness to Light*, frightening a child
in the front row, who has to be carried out,

but exploding into the dance-floor colours of this
converted nave a wave to thrill those of us

perched nervously on the edge. In Ulster
this night three children are set on fire

in a sectarian arson attack. Darkness to
light, the marimba reminds us, glowing its

optimism against the death rattle and attack of
drumkit, Drumcree and deafening Lambeg drums.

Bones

Play the bones

> when the news comes on
> and a voice intones
> the lists of the dead

Play the bones

> when electric chairs
> are restored as thrones
> for a shaven head

Play the bones

> when a lump appears
> and the doctor phones
> but there's still no bed

Play the bones

> when the missiles chew
> on those foreign loans
> that were meant for bread

Play the bones

> when kids online
> turn to making clones
> in the garden shed

Play the bones

> when the battles start
> in tourist zones
> other trade has fled

Play the bones

> when a driver fails
> to observe the cones
> on the months ahead

Play the bones

> when the years stoop
> to pick up stones
> for some words you said

American Music

Samuel Barber asked for croutons to be scattered at his funeral.
From the cortege, as the fresh soil steamed, adagio,
Feldman, Carter, Crumb and all the products of Boulanger
approached to salute and pepper him with their hard pieces.

Bernstein in England

You were New York—even when you performed
Nimrod it was transformed to a traffic jam over
Brooklyn Bridge; and when you at last stormed
Dorabella, she was a West Side lover.

Who was it fell in love with your back?
I watched it writhe through *The Rite of Spring*
when I was a teenager. Tornado-black,
you tore about our hemisphere, could bring

down the Albert Hall with one of your impassioned
rallentandos; and always you enjoyed
a long-drawing-out of pains which others rationed
as liberties. For you, that *Freiheit* was *Freude*.

New World (1937)

The Czech Philharmonic
under Szell
cosying up to
London microphones.

A cor anglais plays
plaintively through
the crackle—a fire
that's just beginning
while the players
like servants to the Lord
Chamberlain wait for it
to catch that piece
of paper waving from
the grate, and shiver.

Even the steady pluck
and gut of their Slavonic
strings can do nothing
but follow the beat
until the bar
where the brass will enter.

Final Transmission

in memory of Charles Greening

I'm sure you're listening, though your headset's gone—
that wreath of wire and bakelite—while I
just have this iPod, playing Wagner by
the Berlin Phil from nineteen forty-one
and peace of sorts. The wartime hiss and drone's
been mastered out: each synchronicity
and near miss, the love motifs, epiphany's
strange star—all gone with the draft. Anon
is free to piece it all together: broken
shellac and blunted thorn. We play at war
with spin and soundbite now; we drop our smart
lies on the bleak, bare facts you might have spoken.
But you had learnt the code, had closed your ears
to all our secrets, knowing them by heart.

Strauss

conducts *Don Quixote*
at the Queen's Hall,
November 1936:

the acetates hiss and clank
like old cattle trucks
over their clickety rails

as the engine pulls them on
to the lyrical uplands—
'Never look encouragingly

at the brass,' he says,
and the wind-machine blows
the steam away into the dark

foggy London air
that he so hates, dreaming
of Garmisch, and the top

brass filing into the front
row seats for the premiere
of his last opera,

and not of the bomb
that will drop on the
Queen's Hall soon.

Death in Aldeburgh

The old friends are assembled in the Red House,
are asked to come and voice a brief farewell,
to pitch him their unbroken pure *laudamus*:
the one whom he blazed out, though she was ill
with nerve disease, the one he brusquely sacked
for questioning the joint imperious will,
the one who had not shown sufficient tact
in telling jokes, the one who stood and eavesdropped
on his practising. All those friendships wrecked
the ebb reveals to him, like small roles grouped
for one of his finales, but not singing,
just smiling, thinking, 'Ben, they never stopped
us loving you, those crushing waves and stinging
rebuffs, that icy undertow, each storm,
each murderous calm. We kept on bringing
our scrofulas for your touch to transform—
and you would rise and glow and wave creation's
spring tide across our skins, your light, your warmth
ripening above these manuscript horizons
to light the steep grey shingle of your moods
and stir our mid-life millpond with your passions.'

Sibelius at Ainola

How do this couple manage to live as two creative artists?
He cannot imagine. One composes, the other sculpts. They live
in harmony, but how much (that dissonance!) his own wife gave
to answer his high calling, how much she sacrificed—a part as

leading lady, to find that now she's only the scullery maid.
The unwritten music of a life she might have led if he
had not reached out to mould her into a silent beauty
bringing his coffee, his cream. She loves his work as much, she said,

as him, and more perhaps. Whenever he writes a courtly masque,
a grand arrival, he wonders what privilege might have been hers;
but it never occurs to him she might have become the creative force
that he (powered by her, of course) now is. Nor will he ask

if she has urges still unsatisfied—a desire to paint
or sculpt, write poetry, or compose. Is it enough to raise
daughters endlessly, to have fostered his genius, and leave hers
beneath the frozen soil, a delicate aristocratic plant

whose scent the world will never catch? She would say 'yes',
and sniff: the source of her husband's art is nobler far than any
ambitions of her own, she has not lived for nothing, no, her destiny
to nurture the word of God, which to her is simply his.

.

As if God had taken the pieces of a mosaic and thrown them down
for him to put together. An impossible jigsaw, his friend once called it,
but the shape would emerge. Take a piece of Italy, of sky, hold it
and think of what you saw in a shaft of sun. Fit the moon,

shining in your brain's dusty hemisphere. Find a star,
some darkness, and see how they might make your missing constellation.
Thus the slow progress of the artist, pulled towards a completion
that does not exist. Even as this one walks among the tesserae,

below the murals (time's march, a creator, the virgin, and waiting
ready a whitewashed wall) outside, the oriole, the thrush, the warbler
call across the Mediterranean. 'All our songbirds are here.
They shoot them, trap them, give them poisoned crumbs. Yet still they sing'.

.

A white-suited spectre, he walks up to his favourite seat
and inspects the landscape. In plain winter sun he simply dazzles,
a presence declaring its territory, warbler among the hazels.
He puzzles over what it was he glimpsed as he stood to greet

his wife when she came downstairs, or as he tuned the wireless
to hear that commemorative broadcast, or while he was at the piano . . .
frames flick by, their specks of dirt and light a continuo
playing as if from the window of a train he is being carried in, fearless

towards the future. Birch, pine, alder. Through a wicket gate
and he's off the heath, back into his thirty years of forest
where every conceivable composition is nesting somewhere, the nearest
storm-battered, the farthest a scrub of lightweight saplings, fit

for domestic consumption only. The man in the white suit, turning
the leaves of his work in his head, a tight smile at his lips and a cigar
unlit before him, thinks what vain creatures we mortals are,
nature will always outwit us, and yet we go on learning.

Greening's long poem about Jean Sibelius, The Silence, *which appears in his 2019 Carcanet collection of the same title, was originally much longer. Prior to publication, however, he cut nearly half the lines on one fateful day. The present poem, in three parts, comprises two sections cut from* The Silence *along with a final passage that survived to appear in the long poem. The first section of the present poem is previously unpublished; the second section was published as 'Sibelius in Italy' in JG's collection,* Moments Musicaux. *The poem 'Sibelius in America,' which appears on p. 206, is another section cut from* The Silence *that same day. KG*

.

One of the Gods

Hoenir longs to speak.

He longs to tell us what Sibelius heard
at Järvenpää, or Bruckner when he knelt to his last finale.

He longs to speak
of what has been written and then forgotten,
of how all things begin and end in silence,
lost or destroyed.

Of Bach beginning to interweave B-flat,
A, C, B-natural
Hoenir longs to speak.

He longs to tell us about the future—

how some will survive the gods' extinction
and nest in golden eaves
and join with the vanished songbirds
to drink the morning dew
                singing of nothing.

from The New English Edda

Orpheus. Eurydice. Hermes

Rilke: 'Orpheus. Eurydike. Hermes'

That was the souls' astonishing deep pit.
They ran like silent veins of silver ore
across its dark. Blood gushed from under roots
and on out to humanity, with a look
as hard as porphyry there in the dark.
Nothing else was red.

But there were cliffs here,
and hazy forests, bridges over nothingness
and that enormous grey blind pond that hung
above its distant depths, a rainy sky
above a landscape. And between meadows
long-suffering, mild, materialised
the one path's pale stripe like a length of washed
white linen laid out.

       On this one path they came.

In front, the lean man in his azure cloak
who looked ahead unspeaking and restless.
His stride devoured the path in hungry chunks,
not chewing them; his hands, leaden, clenched,
hung down out of the falling folds, oblivious
to the lyre striking deep into his left arm
like briar tendrils through an olive tree.
His senses seemed to have been split in two
so that his gaze ran on just like a dog,
turned round, returned, and ran ahead again
and stood waiting at the next blind bend—
while hearing lagged behind like an aroma.
Sometimes it seemed to him his ear did catch
the movement of those other two who should
be following throughout this whole long climb.
But then it cleared into the echo of
his own steps and his own cloak's after-gust.

He told himself they must be coming, though:
said it out loud, and heard it die away.
They must be coming, only
they move, those two, with a dreadful calm.
If he could turn just once (if such a glance
were not wrecking this plot so nearly perfect)
he'd see them, surely, the unruffled pair
behind him, in silence, walking.

       The god
of travel and of distant messages,
a hood pulled down above his brilliant eyes,
a rod held out before him, and his feet
beating rhythmic wings about the ankles,
and there, devoted to his left hand—*she*

who was so loved that from a single lyre
more lamentation came than from lamenting
women, that a world of lamentation
emerged in which all nature rose again:
glen, forest, footpath, village, field, stream, wildlife,
and that around this Lamentation World,
just as around our earth, a sun, a heaven—
stilled and star-filled—was revolving,
a Lamentation Heaven, its stars defaced . . .
she was so loved.

But moved now with that god in hand, her step
restricted by the lengthy winding-sheet,
uncertain, meek, and free of restlessness.
She was sunk in herself like one expectant
and did not think about the man who ran
ahead, nor of the path that climbed to life.
She was sunk in herself, and being dead
filled her like being full.
As full as is a fruit with dusk and sweetness
was she now filled with her own gravid death,
which felt so new she could not grasp anything.

She had entered upon a new virginity
and was unreachable, her sex closed up
like some young flower at evening, and her hands
so unaccustomed to the married life
that even those unendingly so tender
guiding finger touches of the god
pained her like gross familiarity.

She had long ceased to be that blonde-haired girl
who used to echo through the poet's song,
to be the wide bed's fragrance and oasis,
to be that man's belongings, long ceased.

She had already been let down like hair,
been made an offering like fallen rain,
been handed round like an endless abundance.

She had already roots.

And when of a sudden
the god restrained her and in a pained voice
let out the words: *He has turned round*—she could not
take them in, and murmured simply: *Who?*

But far above, dark at the bright way out,
there stood a figure, one whose features were
unrecognisable. He stood and stared
as on the stripe of footpath through a meadow
the god of messages with one sad glance
turned to follow that faint shadow, already
returning down along the track, her step
restricted by the lengthy winding-sheet,
uncertain, meek, and free of restlessness.

Aisling

to Sir Walter Ralegh

We sway,
dark, unrecorded
and beautiful
like bard song
on the air
or like
a selection
of lutes to play
your galliards on.

Our unborn
capering in us
to the rope's jig
at Smerwick—
you, and Grey
and Edmund Spenser
appreciate the dying
fall of
the Irish mothers.

Our lovers
you have taken
to be a consort
of viols and drawn
their guts before
the Fairy
Queen of English
to glib-eyed
silence.

Our language
is mere howling
beyond the pale
wherein
a forty-part
motet of women's
voices plays—
four hundred years
in the unravelling.

William Byrd

in memory of Tessa Bonner

Under a sixty-year-old crab tree, just breaking into blossom,
a girl sings.
         The wind will shake its succession of thorny coronals
but her singing continue.
         It seems I recognise that voice, among others,
a dozen perhaps, who play on somewhere in a garden, in consort,
Byrd, not a mass or anthem now, but 'songs of sundrie natures,
some of gravitie, others of myrth'
         or it might have been Happy Birthday,
that single flame of purity as the day turns wild.
         Follow
the lane for shelter, towards an abandoned farm, a priest hole,
through Butchers Grove, to Heston End.
         Even the nightingales would not
deny her this chance to take on the owls when her voice takes off
for its heavenly note.
         In angels weed, in angels weed, I saw
a noble queen above the skies, in sphere of crystal bright.

Pavan

London 2012

A heathen ground
elaborated by time's
fancy fingerwork—
follow the thread,

the line a lutenist
discovered he could use
to flatter, now cabled
and wound to a shattering.

Are electrical storm
and golden bow
and mysteriously moving
rock a kind of spiritual

opening, or democracy's
shutters? It's Easter.
Though the sun is unwilling
to rise, something earths.

Rhine Journey

The middle stretch is difficult, but I
have kept returning to that long ripe curve
and found it navigable, buoy-marked, safe
for any scribbling Siegfried to get by—
to blow his horn and set out heroically
each day. The middle-aged poet's groove
has dated, while Hildegard, rejuvenated,
sings hologram duets with Lorelei.
The vineyards on the terraces are locked
like monkish books, bound in their cells, loaded
with chants and *Minnelieder* and boredom.
The middle stretch has two sides: one of them—
unless you are a heroine encoded
in a fashionable ring of fire—neglect.

Hildegard

I

A harp that bleeds
Heavenwards. A claw
that scratches out
of the blue. Tentacles.

A rubbery gules
reaching a visionary
sea-bed to finger
the face of an anchoress

who has fixed her eyes
on the leering of her
opposite, poking
his tonsure through cobalt

and watching her supple
movements, ready with
his vellum as she touches
the stylus to her wax

and it almost looks
like a hand-held device
though it swells like a buoyancy
aid from a Rhine cruise.

Invisibly, her toes
are twinkling towards
the scarlet footstool,
its cloven hooves.

II

Taste this Bavarian smoked and now this quark.
Coagulation separates light from dark
into a press of cherub cheesewrights. In their ark,
no rising above the Heaven-set plimsoll-mark,

no herding. But curds and whey. Dominions, thrones,
archangels. And angels dreaming of full moons,
seraphic maturity. Labouring ranks of nuns
in Hildegard's creamery, laying stones.

III

Forty years in one place is long enough
to learn the meaning of peace and thirty
to teach the remorselessness

of war. She moves mountains. To Bingen
where the great gorge begins and although
a salt road is preserved,

the singing of railway lines is the hymn
scheduled today at Rupertsberg since men
dynamited the remains

of her monastery the same year the remains
of her spine, skull and choir cap were first
carried in procession.

IV

Other foundations have been blasted too, blown out
and lost over the Pacific, angel regressing to finch,
then to something demonic, supersonic, or satellite-bearing.

How many revolutions since the English Pope? Since Barbarossa?
Between crusades against a crescent and those on moon dust?
From when life expectancy was what you expected after death?

To evolve. While we in a whirlpool—barges, goods trains,
passenger planes and glazed families—go on revolving.
Then nothing, nothing when it's all gone. The silent,

unaltered rails, herbs on the road, and every trail
vaporised to virgin blue. The Rhine forests are dying
for us to burn or pulp. My daughters have taken their bite

of the Apple. My wife reads about apparitions at Versailles.
My sister, I search for illuminations in your *Scivias*:
the great dark star, the cosmic egg, God's wheel.

Intimations

The Orchard

Passing by an orchard at a distance
the trees may be seen to grow in lines
certain inches at certain times

but climbing over the stile
that separates the road from the trees
where the speed limit drops

and winding down my windows
that are misted up with travelling
I see now:

the orchard is unholily tangled,
and the details of the action
are a progression of doubt,
faith into doubt.

The monodic trunk
breaks into couples half as strong
and into families and relationships
weakening into stick-orgies
and twigs
so high they snap.

This is the logical consequence
of the binary system
where the choice is yes or no.

In the end so many apples
blush out of the confusion,
the tree trunk must bend,
and as the owners
shake, pick, pull down and justify
the fruit
into an ecstasy of cider
the tree trunk overloads.

In the orchard there are many stumps.
Sheep graze around them,
and boys scrumping
stand in the ancient circles
and reach from the dry memory banks
into the sticks' flow diagram
for a conclusive eater,
suspended somewhere
on two twigs that make an equals sign.

On those stumps they won't reach it.

A blackbird
deep in the tree's darkest fractions
pecks all the eaters
and sings.

Brampford Speke, Devon,
March 1977

Dornröschen

A walk along the field edge,
the hedgerow full of half-seen
imagery and instinct, is what the night
feels like as you wake from it—

the night that blank, flat, ploughed
extent where anything might exist
or nothing, the dream the one barrier
between you and oblivion—

follow that last hedge into the yawning
east, follow its elm and ash,
its blackthorn, hawthorn, briar, traveller's
joy and fruit-flowering spindle.

Power Lines

No Huntingdon White Horse, no feature carved by Grim
or dropped by the Devil, no Tor where Alfred or Arthur might
have sat, no headless pack of hounds, no Dragon—

but a solitary antlered figure that seems to have leapt
from a Palaeolithic cave wall in France, prancing
across the eastern English landscape like a hobby-horse,

to the steps of a dance that has even inspired the wind
to a composition, and which it has sketched in starlings
on the horizon: *Oss, oss, wee oss!* it sings to itself

at winter sunset. Or when the stubble burning is in progress,
it crackles and strides between the dying fires like
a druid wicker man. But on schoolday afternoons, it looks

a procession of bare facts through the classroom window:
the progress of power; Cromwell's Ironsides about to charge;
Queen Catherine's funeral cortege draping the county.

First dawn of the holidays, I was out walking through
one of those islands of scrub kept solely for the game
and saw a sudden flash that I took to be roe or fallow,

but as I moved to where it had been, it became a skeleton,
man-made and erect. There is nothing at all ghostly about
a pylon—grey folded arms, the sheen of gunmetal—yet

home, I lit at once our little stag-headed altar:
the images flickered comfortingly as I lay chained by
my imagination, a landscape barbed with the literal.

from Huntingdonshire Eclogues

Gidleigh, 1974

for Stephen Hanvey

No room at the hostel.
At least there's one bed
and with some pleading
a couch in the lobby
of this simple dwelling
on the edge of Dartmoor.

Before it grows dark, I spot
the carvings on the couch—
weird beast heads, gargoyles—
then yawn good night, shut
the door that opens
directly on to Dartmoor,

turn off the light and sink
down, exhausted after
our day's trek between
red triangles across
the loneliest, most Grimpen
stretches of Dartmoor.

But I am pulled up out
of sleep by something
plucking at my feet.
I stumble, fumble for
the light beside the closed
door out on to Dartmoor,

then fall back, imagining
it must have been a cat,
it must have been a dream,
starting to drift, only to be
shaken awake by voices,
music rising off Dartmoor

as if, somewhere out there
where there is no house,
there were a party in
full swing. And more,
I realise the light between
me and the dark of Dartmoor

that was on is now
off or that was off
is now on, and as the echoes
die and as the claws in
my imagination retract, I
am left to sense Dartmoor

pushing at the door of
consciousness, trying to
persuade me of its alibis
and its forced confessions
of all I have been educated
to overlook. Dartmoor

smiles as the sun comes up,
and my friend smiles,
the pack of scouts in the
other room smile. I look
for clear lines on the map
to help us laugh off Dartmoor.

An Offering

We live on the dry surface,
power our grass short
and play over rich topsoil.
Keep a cap on the old wells,

afraid to imagine what might echo
under familiar place names, or what
if we should stop turning
and pull, and lift the concrete.

My offering to the guardians
of the thousand covered wells
lost to mucilage, or filled
with hardcore and paved, my gift

to St. Anne, to Black Annis,
to you nymphs and water deities,
to all trout, snakes, toads, flies
that guard them still, is these

lines that are bent like steel
wishing pins—catch them!—words
spin-gleaming through your legendry,
new-coined; and if you have no wish

for this severed head that sings
its vaporous red trail
down into your nursery rhymeless
black, toss it back.

Old Shuck

where the cloudscape is a parade of vapour trails and blue ideas

where the horizon fizzes to its power lines of poplar and spire

where the windmills prop themselves like armless puritan soldiers

where the church quivers as a bog oak heaves from the grave

where the ditches lure young drivers with their murky pheromones

where the peat shrinks from silver tracks as they press their advance

the black dog sits

Fox

While you were studying Greek
(but was it Aesop?)
he hurled himself twice
at the french window

like some revolutionary
in a Hall of Mirrors,
alarming the cat, enthroned
on his usual sofa.

Had he mistaken our den
of books for the portal
to a parallel world of ecto-
plasmic chickens?

Or was he trying in a fury
of personal conviction
to attack some rival glimpsed
in his own reflection?

You watched him saunter past
my shelves of Hughes
and Tomlinson, confused,
but thoughtful, towards

the hawthorn, which he jumped
with a quick look
back, sour grapes
on his red face.

Night Calls

Our local doctor
tells of his horror
of owls

of how they will gaze
surgically into your
soft tissue

from the far side of
their barred habitat
their spell of solitary

or wing into your beams
on the way to a
head-on crash

they hoot like doom's
emergency service
and they stand

rubber-necking in the fog
when motorway
madness strikes

their shrieks are the new-
born dead
taking to the darkness

Nocturne

Owl season. I lie in bed and think of the dead,
think of that curdling cry in the middle of the day
before my father died. And of one that was brought into

a Camelford pub just as my 'Night Calls' was published.
It was carried over to us, we were invited to stroke it.
George Macbeth, crippled by motor neurone, lives

in his owl poem. John Haines, the voice of Alaska,
leaves his owl mask in this dreamer's way
one day we are heading for Deception Pass. And now

at the World Owl Centre, survivors of *Aufklärung*
interned in concentration gaze at that fell
where late romanticism crawled. The eaves are gone

that the barn owls used to haunt—our lane's last
barn collapsed and took four centuries with it—
but the mews, hoots and screeches, they shake us nightly.

The Rose Window

Rilke: 'Die Fensterrose'

Inside, the slow patrolling of their paws
enforces a disorientating calm,
but then the violence of that great high gaze
will stray occasionally to where they roam,

these feral cats, who have to take it on,
a gaze that seems itself to be possessed
by forces whirling gradually down
until it sinks into forgetfulness,

this eye, which first you'd think is safely dormant,
opens, then shuts, half starting to erupt,
digging its claws until it just draws blood.

So once upon an after-dark age moment
the great rose windows of the cathedrals ripped
a heart out, tore it straight on into God.

Rosslyn

'Of what is past, or passing, or to come'

Something said do not go into the temple.
Was it those Green Men, a hundred and ten
at least, hidden among the stone carvings
like songbirds camouflaged in a hedgerow?

One sticks his tongue out at your walking stick
as you creep in like an apprentice before
the sorcerer. *Feed us, and we will tell you all.*
We hope for scallops, but a snail or a worm . . .

And others come babbling in canonical
parts a chant that would raise the chapel roof
(*Feed us!*) if money had not already turned
gold to base metal for our enlightenment.

We are prophets who survived Byzantium
and migrated here to find new Lords and Ladies
in need of guidance. Outside, old mines, a grey
kirk, the macadamised road, then a path

that plunges druidically to real birds
singing from real oak trees (*Ishtar, Ishtar,*
they twitter, *Isis . . .*) and into the leafy
mouth of a gorge where there are no compasses.

'The Heathen Stones'

Hard to take in, even to look at, in this cold:
the set of a lost film, colourless, it stands
dreaming Preseli, all healing powers
frozen out of it, unable to advise
whether the sun will even rise, and ignorant
of beards and mistletoe. No one today
treads a straight path towards Stonehenge,

though these from China go on zooming
as if they were touching, and America's pilgrim
sons reach out as if they might
convert to BC. But all of us
obey English Heritage's rule and follow
a snake of beanies, quilts and thinsulate
down the pre-school underpass—turn

into zoo creatures circling a prey
already killed, only looking up
in mock concentration as we're urged
round the track, a grim and shabby orbit.
On either side of the wire the world goes on
ignoring what's going on, accelerates
into the west, out of this terrible cold.

Terminal

If as you tap your reg in the car parking machine
the number that appears ends in BC

If as you take the Tube from Hatton Cross to the terminal
others in your cage have obvious tattoos

If as you look at the departures board you realise your flight
from the Palaeolithic has been delayed

If as you book into the Temporal Inn and give your name
the name that comes out is Hundes

If as you lay your head on to memory foam the pillow
turns to an anvil, your dream to flint

If as you reach in the bathroom for the shower gel you find instead
a small green amulet of a boar

If as your taxi arrives it has a skull swinging at the glass
and a driver singing 'Circle of Life'

If as you're taken through the underpass you think you see
mistletoe in a canopy of oak boughs

If as the uniforms look you over they find in your baggage
a sickle, a celt and a bronze gouge

If as a last something for the journey they press a cold
shoulder of mutton into your hand

If as the procession slithers through a silver barrier
towards a grove of tinted glass

If as a clearing opens in the old heath and the plain
facts dawn on you, especially

If as they greet you the stewards are in white or bearded and say
welcome to Rune Air . . . then ask

if fares from Hounslow Heath are perhaps refundable

Study, January 2021

No mountain here, Cézanne. A tangle
of box, privet, flowering currant,
and plants I can't identify.
The dead of winter, very Anglo-
Saxon damp and mist, an errant
sun, distressed grey sky.

Pigeons patter across the slate,
a blue tit pecks the window sill,
our neighbour's cutting something down.
The radio's repeats repeat
echoes from 2020's tunnel
till even the light at the end has gone.

A flying saucer seems to hover
outside among the birch and holly:
translucent yellow through the glass.
A passing alien observer?
Some herald angel bringing holy
bulletins of change? Alas,

it's just my study light reflected,
though strange enough to conjure thoughts
beyond the here and now, illusion
of other lives, of unexpected
gifts from interested gods.
A trick—but so is television,

Pandora would point out, so shut
the door on strangeness, check your sense
of smell, and take whatever action
science tells you to. Since art
has failed to leap to life's defence,
we'll hug this lid for our protection.

For St Martin's

It's clear that the trousers ordered from China, thick as a blanket,
for wearing on her early morning litter-picking circuit
(with a torch and some lines about Diogenes) are unfit

for purpose, made for someone smaller, for guarding the Great
Wall of China, perhaps. She thinks they would suit
a homeless person and recalls the London charity (too late

for Christmas, but still), packs them up, and wants to add
an accompanying note. So she grabs an old card,
begins to write, 'Please . . .' when she sees what's portrayed:

a stained glass window from Angers, and printed above
St Martin partageant son vêtement avec un pauvre.
'St Martin dividing his cloak in two in order to give

to a poor man.' Gods of coincidence, who ignore
reason and walls and other objections, may you ensure
such threads of humanity reach St Martin's door.

from Huntingdonshire Codices

Wind

Invisible hand that jangles the lantern over the porch
and tells the leaves on the pond to imagine they are clippers
and wrenches the shed door, and makes leylandii lurch,
unnerving the cat, wobbling the elderly; that viciously clobbers
pedestrians at the corner, then snatches up bills and payslips
put out for recycling and juggles with them; that gibbers
and squeaks through gaps in your sealed units; that laughs as it swipes
her portfolio of art, the pantechnicon of his life's work, in fits
when a cone skidaddles like a clown or turning Dalek wipes
the smile off its fierceness and swivels a death-ray that hits
your moped, your chimney, your safest nook, knocking over
five centuries' peaceful growth. It is its own blitz-
krieg on the establishment. Respect it. Let it recover
equilibrium—be patient—let it blow itself out
and lie quietly, a champion featherweight, a winged lover.

Renewable

Up here is where Broadview wants to harvest wind
(of which the Urals ensure a surfeit) unconcerned
that it's also the base from which America chose to send

Flying Fortresses on bombing raids, that here marks
the place where some came back to stay. These concrete tracks
we use for jogging, walking the dog, riding our bikes,

were what they limped towards, their last approach
in line with the weather-cock on the spire of St Andrew's Church,
whose bell today announces time. A sign in the porch

warns of incoming turbines. Think of history.
Think of natural beauty. No one mentions the mystery
of those helmeted aircrew on the tracks. It's just a story.

But we've known people who are clear what they have seen.
Yes, wind power is rational, economical, clean,
but there are other sources to tap, have always been.

from Huntingdonshire Codices

On the Runway

A man has been spotted standing on the runway, looking
anxiously as if he were waiting for the Tube, although
the Tube will not be leaving Hounslow for years.
Flights have been grounded, security is on its way,
but he's unmoved, intent on looking, looking
for his briefcase, this best-dressed scarecrow, unscared
by lasers, acoustic dispersal, or hi-vis waving
(*Clear off—people are wanting their holidays, there are
urgent supplies for Africa, VIPs
in the lounge, animals in the hold!*). Where is that missing
combination lock, whose number he knows so well
he can repeat it, repeat it . . . ? A honking red
and orange v comes smearing by to flash
and grab the scene, and hisses right through him.

Of course, he was never there. An urban myth
drifting through our online departure lounge,
materialised from something in 1948,
a crash, or some other rubbish from the '70s.

But I knew that man. He walked out on to the Heath
one morning in his grey flared suit,
his sandwiches safe in their tupperware, and disappeared
into the rising sun, took off, was gone,
his paunch, moustache and sideburns, his cigarette smoke,
and in his briefcase—what? Not, one imagines,
a report on the latest findings regarding the percentage
of people in terminal buildings who might be ghosts.

In the Castle

Typing up on the top floor of the Tudor castle
I used to teach in, typing pages of old verse
for some collection I dreamt of, trying to pass

the late evening shift's long final hour,
typing on a better computer than mine, hoping to store
the text on its hard drive. One page more

of the dozens, it's a sestina: 'For the Six Wives',
elaborate piece of artifice compressing their lives
into six verses (and an envoi). No one believes

this place where she died is really haunted, but typing away
I reached the passage where I'd written about the day
of Catherine's funeral, how Anne Boleyn . . . and, as I say,

there are no ghosts. But at the line, the word, 'Anne',
the computer crashed. I typed it again. It crashed, and then
the poem simply vanished. I exited. I ran.

from Huntingdonshire Codices

A Dream

The night my father died, I had a dream of flying—
not above those ivory fields, crop-marked with silver
hoards and tesserae: this entered through the Gate of Horn.

And I didn't know, as I slept, that he was lying dead.
A crowded sky, a buoyancy of purpose, a welcoming or guiding
upwards of something or someone . . . Lost. Yet, Mozart could summon

Allegri intact from that one *Miserere* in the Sistine Chapel.

from Huntingdonshire Nocturnes

Ultima Thule

Betty Greening, née Turner
born May Whale, 1926
died November 2007

Beyond the Blitz
and your mother's bi-
polar meltdown,
beyond the twice
breaking waters'
book of hours,
your polymyalgia,
angina, stroke,

you pull through
stiff breakers,
a last Viking
queen, crested
motionless against
the sea drift
towards your own
Ultima Thule.

Laid in a flow
of white, masked
below a dripping,
hissing cairn,
you shift at each
waft and call
and quake of the bed's
tectonic plates.

Now your yellow
pod begins
to shoot and force
its pale poisons
sunwise, where
the Iceland poppy
trembles in a de-
compressed breeze.

Here is where you
wait to meet
your hidden one
who's listening at
the tunnel end of
the tube, who might
have lost you between
stations on a night

once, northbound
into a shadow land,
a last encryption
beyond the hanging
whispers and dark
adoption myths,
the unrooted
family tree—

breathing ever
more distantly,
the Arctic opening
its circle to you,
where the whale
blows that sailed
away with your
birth name.

The Norns

Between my word-hoard and the house
a well is sunk, an ash tree grows.
The tree marks where a hedge was lost;
its trunk is bent, its branches quest
for strength and straightness of a spear.
The well has been in camera
a century or more: it yawns
down sixteen feet and only coins
a rhyme when its wooden cover slides
to show where that old woman hides
who threw herself in, years ago.
But why, and who she was . . . ? Below
the ash tree are three women: Fate,
Necessity and Being. Light
falls from my wooden house of words
across night's wapentake towards
a well that we choose not to fill,
a tree that I refuse to fell.

Urðr

To wit, as you came down, prepared
to write these lines, your wireless blared
Tchaikovsky's Fate motif. Mere chance
or meaningful coincidence?
Don't ask what causes what, but find
(the Chinese tell you this) which kind
of things like to occur with which.
Inspecting then the complex stitch
of your past life here tapestried,
consult my pocket guidebook: Weird
for Amateurs. Ask, was it all
so random—when you made that call
or took that turning, traced that line?
Someone is writing you. They sign
themselves into your every deed.

Your plot may be far-fetched, but read
the next page . . . Ah, the bye-laws say
you can't do that unless you pay
with health or youth, with hairs or years.
It makes no difference. Fate still blares
as you trip wittily downstairs.

Verðandi

Live for the now—you never know
what's round the corner. There they go,
the post-Christmas ramblers, old
or middle-aged, confronting cold
and aches and gloom to walk ten miles
through clinging clay, over broken stiles,
across their barbed anxieties
to charge that solar-powered 'is'.
Walk your circle. Live for the day
like kids in blissful unwatched play.
Haydn seeks the key in a bright
C major presto. Let in light.
And may it last throughout the night.
Joke how your own long middle age
would once have been the final page
or even an appendix (or
the index of first lines). Live for
the now, you never know what's round
the corner, dark untrodden ground.

Skuld

You'd so much like to read this page.
I see a name here. And an age.
The cause of death. A brief account
of life and works. It won't amount

to more than one side, but it's all
one needs to know. When ash keys fall,
can you predict where they will land?
Or which will germinate? It's planned,
the spin, the sprouting, etched in rings
of Yggdrasil and fed from springs
of deepest Urð. Necessity:
the law that what must be must be.
You so desire to catch these words
whistling overhead, black birds
that gather high up out of sight
and hide their tone rows from the light
and turn their dark keys on the air.
But would you truly want to hear
that raven aria, your Farewell,
a Ring of Fire, the road to Hel,
the Bridge collapsing, Godhead go
into the wolf's jaws? Curtain. No,
better face my glacial block
on urges reaching beyond the clock
than know the words of Ragnarok.

*In Norse mythology, the three women known as Norns control human destiny. They live beneath
the gods' endangered World Tree, the ash Yggdrasil, which they water (thus bringing dew to earth).
They are shadowy figures, but their arrival clearly spells the end of the gods—so-called Ragnarok,
as suggested in the apocalyptic poem, "Völuspá" (see "Coming Soon," p. 262). JG*

The Scarab

Rilke: 'Der Käferstein'

Are you not within reach of the stars,
and what keeps you from that change of sphere
when you can't even seem to grasp these cores
of carnelian, the scarab beetles here

without the zone that holds their elytra
in place pressing your own whole
blood to the limit; never was that outer
mystery closer, more yielding. Its pull

has been with these scarabs for millennia, still
unbroached, forever in a steady state,
and they close their beetle selves, free-fall
asleep to the rocking of its zero weight.

To the Sun

after Akhenaten

Glorious as the hills in the east now
it spills light, at sea level.

Feast from its prehistoric silver
plate, these dateless riches,

released at last from the tyranny
of sunlessness, of light starvation.

A distant fact, an elephant-in-the-room
dictator, retiring, then flaring

beyond the trace of any probe,
we forget you, plugged into our

electric shadow, drowning in dazzling
gloom, asleep under sodium,

among coiled, low-energy dreams:
we dare not look at one another

unless it's through a screen, strangers
steal our identities, friends become

spot, rash, stroke . . . feverish,
we forget that you have even set

and are rising already over Al-Hadr,
the swastika lands, the dragon cities,

the thorny paths of Wuriupranili.
But dawn comes, though we ignore its

sacred polyphony, an alarm call
from *Star Trek*, the kettle boiling, cars

as they tick, the radio chatter:
it will be hot, there will be flights

towards your smile, which says *I am here
behind ceiling tiles, rafters,*

*insulation, slates and slaty rain-
clouds, beyond volcanic ash.*

*Bathe, bask, bare all, ride
your chariot, let us be gas guzzlers,*

*my fingers touching that prominence
to bless your bones and infiltrate*

the days, the years. And do not raise
the subject *x*, the item *gamma*

as we apply the UV cream to our children
by the sea, and do not listen to what follows

the pips (the fission, ozone, carbon
dioxide, fusion and confusion).

Let the chick come unmutated
from the egg. Let it come crowing.

Crops must be warm. We must put up
with polytunnels. Keep the cliffs secure,

till desert and its wildfires stagger
over the horizon. Respect the winter,

don't give your smouldering horses
rein such as will hurl us all

to a solar arc. You watched us rise.
Don't let us be washed away

in rolling news. We do not understand
the gravity of your stare, the currents

above or below, we simply know
time and tide, it never rains,

make hay, the switch that says on/
off. We block, we quit the field.

The turbines begin to turn, but you
are the only god we believe in, even here

in East Anglia: as on the West Bank.

Coda

Aufklärung

'Do you mean, sir, there are 104 symphonies by Haydn like this one?'
   H. C. Robbins Landon, quoted in the Daily Telegraph *obituary, November 2009*

Something to raise the spirits, to lighten the dark times—   1
a day remembered, a kindness, the music of Haydn, and rhyme's
pleasing close encounters. We're used to crossing the street
by now to avoid a friend, to greeting that blurred sheet
of perspex in Budgens, to washing our hands obsessively   5
from morning (as the Business News announces how massively
Netflix and Amazon are profiting) through midday (when
we gather up the post) and into evening, again
and again, then rinsing the shopping. Because we are enlightened,
simply do as we're told, determined not to be frightened   10
at Rumour's tongues. But how does Time expect us to endure . . . ?
By listening, watching, reading. By planting a hundred and four
ways to get you through, and tapping their green cure
like those seedlings our daughter has started to nurture on her terrace,
a WhatsApp shot of them each day. But also like worries   15
that squirm to reach the light. It's true we're almost resigned
to confinement, our little pot of minor: the walk around
the block, speaking for once, maybe, to someone new
who's lived across the lane for years, a doctor who
works in A&E. And when we go out to applaud   20
key workers, that's a shift to major. Would you have allowed
bin collectors or nurses into your Republic, Plato,
since poets didn't make it? And would you perhaps care to
remark on the effect of being left in your cave to watch
shadows flickering at us since the Ides of March?   25
Alack and welladay. We survive. They've closed the church,
but there are quizzes—every Sunday on our conference call.
'Reflections' was the last week's theme: they got them all
except our one about the Lady of Shalott, half-sick
of quarantine. Hallelujah, and the mirror's crack   30

has put her back in touch. A horn call. Camelot—
though not quite as she'd dreamt it. I trust our ending
won't be via funeral barge. I have been sending
emails to old friends (the emphasis on 'old')
since they're the ones who when they turn to face the world   35
are most at risk. Some won't even make it online
to search half-snowblind until midnight for a way in
to Iceland, as we did. An echo asks me how my father
would have coped, who spent those two years in another
spell of lockdown: Akureyri, in that wireless hut's   40
darkness—it got to him, I think. And my mother's Blitz?
That's not (although it is) so different. Look up, and it's
a starry night in London, a planet near the sun
is searing her inside, but she is mourning one
beyond the icy reaches. Fare well. Their cortege   45
passes through that archway into peace, and we emerge
from *Sturm und Drang*, with ringing ears and rationed food,
imperious, prepared never to have had such good
health now the pillars have fallen, all passion spent.
Living with less, acquiring more, it's swiftly learnt.   50
History says we must wash our vision clean, predicts
a date as indelible as 1665 (or 6).
The empire of assumptions starts to shrink to a commonwealth
of compromise, pared circumstance. And a birth,
unexpected, as if a teacher suddenly turned   55
a cartwheel in front of the class. Just now he had warned
us about our behaviour, said we were all in danger
of being kept in. At school, I was bell-ringer
(marking the lesson's end with a sound like the start of a fire)
so could wander distractedly out as if unaware   60
that a grim calculation was spreading from desk to desk.
I'd close the door and *BRRRING*. Now, I want to ask
a question of my own. Too late. Becalmed. Nothing but rocks
and a light that keeps on flashing, whether to warn or coax
is not so clear. A voice in my head insists it's a hoax.   65

But how can we escape it? We are not Doctor Who,
can't slip into our box and head for, I don't know,
Eisenstadt, or even the London of the future
when this will all have become an exam: 'What was the nature
of the crisis at the beginning of the twenty-first century?'   70
They went on serving the old Prince. Eventually
it dawned on them how things could change, that there were trophies
of another kind beyond their walls, out in the leafy
suburban wilds where birds, it seemed, were coming back,
the cuckoo, lapwings, tiny piercing things, and the bleak   75
horizon sang: blue skies, clear air.
The carbon they never managed to capture wasn't there.
Instead they found a future. Children. From Trafalgar Square
to the High Dam at Aswan, from Athens to Hampton Court,
the vine renewed its mazy growth. But always the thought   80
of those behind the yew hedge in their toxic trance—
like the thought of a bear on a chain that is tortured to make it dance,
like the thought of a hen in its cage that pecks at its only chance.
So we turn on the box for the briefing, the update, to hear the PM
or the Queen reassure us that everything's really just the same   85
old game of Happy Families. Keep back the bad
news by playing the good Mum or perfect Dad
in the latest streamed box set on Zoom. So it plays
unstoppably, day's slow introduction, phrase
by interminable phrase; a burst of cheerful light   90
develops; the slow mid-morning; teatime minuet
that trips so gracefully from Oxford into Cambridgeshire
and finally, the summing up. And always be prepared
for the Surprise. A gift hung on your gatepost. The clip
in your inbox you instantly share. The online quip. The hope   95
of a miracle that momentarily flashes on your screen,
swells and fades. You are the mariner who knows he's been
aboard the *Marie Celeste* and lived: what matters
is making it back to Enlightenment through these dark waters
as if they were sending you home from a war, to measure each day   100

like a clock, *not yet, not yet*. And say
convincingly: soon (yes, soon) we are going to wake to hear
a drumroll crescendo, it's about to end, about to clear
the way for you to London or beyond. You can disappear.   104

Stonely, Cambridgeshire,
13th May 2020

An Interview with John Greening

Thank you so much for allowing me to explore with you the sources of your poetry. When did you first know that you wanted to write poetry, that the Muse had her eye on you?

It certainly began early, though if the Muse visited, she came in the rather forbidding form of my headmistress at primary school, who hauled me into her study to congratulate me on a poem titled "Jehoshaphat Jim and Jehoshaphat Joe." I must have been 8 or 9. I had always been drawn to rhymes, and whenever we went on vacation I would produce an illustrated verse journal. In fact, I won a national prize for one about our school holiday to the Wye Valley, near Tintern Abbey. I'm not sure what Wordsworth would have thought of my doggerel, which was all written in the voice of my duffel bag.

Poems written from the perspective of inanimate objects are rare enough, but I would venture to guess that yours is the only poem ever written in the voice of a duffel bag! Let's circle back to persona poems and dramatic monologues a bit later. Can you tell me about the first poem you published, when you knew, this is it, I've truly written a poem that I'm proud of?

There were several early attempts I must have felt pleased with, including one never published (nor will it be) about the Pyramids. Writing it made me suddenly realise what poetry could do. This was years before we actually went to live in Upper Egypt, where I would find something like a satisfactory poetic "voice," stimulated by the place and the upheaval in our lives. I must have been sixteen or so, and it was a long-lined affair comparing the transience of butterflies to the immemorial stones of Giza. All very contrived. My first mature, publishable poem (there had been hundreds of immature ones) was written while standing in an orchard in the village of Brampford Speke, near Exeter, in March 1977. The orchard was attached to the bungalow where I was living with two other postgrads. It was a beautiful spot, highly inconvenient for the university, but within reach of Dartmoor (once I had acquired a secondhand Honda 50 moped) and wonderfully atmospheric. The village itself boasted a pub called The Agricultural Inn, which consisted of an elderly woman's front parlour. Our bungalow was a cheaply built "tied cottage" perched on the banks of the Exe, which during the winter rose right up to just below the window ledge of the tiny bedroom I occupied on the far side. That was something to watch, undoubtedly, if only for the sake of self-preservation. But it was the orchard that I particularly loved. On the day I wrote the poem, I remember willing myself to look attentively, not looking through, but at. I wanted to convey precisely what I was seeing, which in March cannot have been apples, yet for all its symbolism the poem does suggest scrutiny of the actual tree. I can still recall the feeling that at last I was in touch with the real source of poetry, that the more I looked the more I seemed to be watching something other than the tree come into bud. "The Orchard" was published in the rather prestigious tabloid-style literary magazine, *Bananas*, edited by Emma Tennant, a fact which would impress Ted Hughes when we corresponded that year (I didn't know at the time he had been conducting an affair with her, as related in her memoir, *Burnt Diaries*). "The Orchard" was one of my first published poems, but I've never reprinted it until now. Perhaps I should have had more faith in my 23-year-old self.

It's wonderful to have this poem printed again, after all these years, and I'm honored you'd allow me to reprint a work so personal and meaningful to you. You wrote "The Orchard" while you were a postgraduate at Exeter in the '70s. How did your work toward your MA prepare you for the poet you have become?

I was preoccupied with writing plays at that time. I had already caused consternation at Swansea by handing in *Ragnarok* (about Norse mythology) instead of facing the usual first-year exam, and at Exeter my dissertation was on verse drama—though the stage production of my next play (*Schumann*) rather dominated my year there. It should perhaps have taught me how little I understood of the dramatist's art, but that would take another quarter of a century. I learnt more, I think, from the wonderful letters I had from Ted Hughes, who lived near Exeter, after I cheekily sent him my *Three Devon Plays*. He gave me all kinds of advice in very Hughesian terms—for example, that as a playwright I should prepare to be publicly crucified. He also advised me not to teach, which I spectacularly ignored.

You certainly did. You spent many years teaching in a variety of settings, though mostly in a posh public school—or what we'd term a private school . . .

Yes, isn't that confusing. I also went to a grammar school, which means something different in the US. Teaching at Kimbolton was certainly easier than teaching in Aswan, where I faced classes of fifty in rooms with unglazed windows, often with no textbooks and only a painted wall for blackboard.

Did teaching influence your writing in any way? Or hinder it?

Sometimes writing was a way of escaping the teaching. It was helped by the fact that my colleague was the poet Stuart Henson, so we could chat about what was going on in the poetry world. There had been quite a tradition of poets teaching at the school—Neil Powell, for instance. At one time in the UK, before creative writing departments appeared, it was perfectly normal for poets to be high-school teachers, and other than going into advertising there weren't many alternatives. Ted Hughes, Charles Causley, Iain Crichton Smith, Wendy Cope . . . they were all schoolteachers at one time. No, my school was within walking distance of home and in congenial surroundings (a haunted Tudor castle!) and there were generous holidays so I had plenty of time to write, even if it sapped my energy. Stuart and I used to muse on the fact that fatigue might actually be creative. I enjoyed teaching generally, and always found I learnt things about literature from my pupils, however young they were. They would notice details I had missed entirely. It was a great opportunity to try out my own plays with older students, too, though I also put on Chekhov, Václav Havel, John Whiting—oh, and my colleague Steve Pollard and I staged a mammoth production of *Oh, What a Lovely War!* with a cast of a hundred. I taught for a year at Bridgewater High in New Jersey, too, on a Fulbright exchange. We swapped houses and jobs with an American couple, Franklin and Judy Harris, and we all had a great time, though I think we had the better bargain as their house was enormous. It was there I wrote what is probably my best verse drama, *A Ladder in Hopewell*, about the Lindbergh kidnap. There are some poems you have selected from that time too, several previously uncollected. I hope readers won't feel I was being too presumptuous—there are many things I'm sure I don't quite "get" about America. Oddly enough, I wrote some of my most English pieces while in New Jersey—"Under the Flight Path," for instance, and "For the Six Wives." On an electric typewriter, I seem to recall.

How do you usually write? What are your writing habits?

I am one of those pencil addicts. Lots of drafts—twenty, thirty—and then typing up, at which point there's further on-screen revision. The usual rule is that just as I've turned off the computer I think of something I should have changed! And I'm normally working much of the day out in our so-called "word-house": a wooden shed full of books and manuscripts, built of necessity when we outgrew our tiny mid-terrace cottage. It's quite peaceful, except when a neighbour decides (as now) to build a swimming pool. I like early mornings, while dreams are still within reach, although as I've said, a weary evening session can sometimes produce good results.

You've mentioned Hughes as an early influence. Besides him, who were some other early influences? What poets do you most admire or find yourself rereading most frequently over the years?

Hughes is a dangerous model; you find your poetry is suddenly full of dark similes and random screams. I don't think many of those poems have found their way into this selection, I'm relieved to say. I came gradually to prefer the more controlled, restrained voices among contemporary poets (Charles Tomlinson, say, or Eavan Boland), but I have catholic tastes, including many Americans as I have discussed in my Preface. Yeats has been very important to me from the start, but it's Eliot who has gone deeper, especially his *Four Quartets* as you shrewdly note in your introduction. I began by picking blindly, discovering the diverse delights of Kamau Brathwaite, Edith Sitwell, Robert Creeley, Denise Levertov, Norman Nicholson. Only gradually did anything like a canon become clear; it was just a personal anthology of favourites. That is still rather the way I read. One day I can't get enough Pope, the next it's my beloved Wordsworth. And I return endlessly to the sixteenth and seventeenth centuries. George Gascoigne I couldn't do without, and I am always discovering new writers from that period. I'm currently relishing the light touch and sheer humanity of Charles Cotton. Then there are all the foreign poets dismissed by Larkin (who himself was enormously influential—I had much of *High Windows* in my head at one stage) such as Rilke, Szymborska, Seferis and Cavafy.

Thinking of early influences, your first full-length collection is about Egypt, and Egypt is a subject that continues to resurface in your work. What sort of influence has Egypt had on your developing imagination?

A profound influence, and I've written about it in my memoir *Threading a Dream: A Poet on the Nile.* But it wasn't only the place; it was also what I was reading while we lived there. All those Imagists, for example, and so much William Carlos Williams—that's probably obvious from the shape of the pieces you've selected. The poems in *Westerners* were an expression of the sheer excitement of being in Upper Egypt from 1979 to 1981 (there were very few Europeans there at the time) and I was jotting things down almost as one might take photos—and I refused to take actual photos partly because the poems were doing that for me. I sent them home to my father to submit to magazines and they were some of my earliest published poems. At the same time I was learning about form. A reading of Louis MacNeice's *Autumn Journal* (it's surprising what we could get hold of through the British Council library) prompted the *terza rima* of "The Crack," for example. And there's a response to Shelley's "Ozymandias" which you've picked out—that hasn't been in print since 1982. I still believe in these poems, and perhaps they have worn better than some from my "middle stretch," to use MacNeice's phrase, so I'm happy that you like them too. Winning the Alexandria International Poetry Prize in 1981 was quite a finale to two extraordinary years, and a personal confirmation that I was doing something right—though it was distinctly odd to be receiving the award from Jehan Sadat on the site of the Pharos, one of the Wonders of the Ancient World. Egypt gave me my voice, undoubtedly, and I've usually thought of it as where it all began, but collaborating on this selection has made me see things rather differently.

Would you say more about that?

I think those two years just brought out what had already begun to emerge during some years of fairly conventional church-going. The Ancient Egyptians knew a thing or two about the afterlife, and it seems to me that this crucial area is the one that the modern Church (not to mention modern poetry) has rather overlooked. Yet poets who have dabbled in spiritualism tend to be ignored or they are mocked for it, as Yeats was. In fact, Yeats's poetry is inseparable from his belief in magic. Do I believe in magic? I used to be a (very bad) children's conjuror, so I understand entirely why Harry Houdini spent his life trying to debunk it; but I have also had personal experiences which can only be called truly magical. I'm a Jungian at heart, so I always try and remain alert to such things—especially to coincidence, to what Les Murray called that essential "doubleness." One of the reasons I gave my 2008 collection, *Iceland Spar*, that title is because it's a mineral that makes everything appear double, and even the Sibelius of *The Silence* is partly a mask for JG.

From desert sands to ice and volcanoes: I want to circle back to Iceland. But can we theorize for a moment? I've wondered if you'd define yourself as a poet of place. Two English regions recur with great frequency in your poems—Hounslow Heath and Huntingdonshire. How have you managed to avoid becoming a regional poet?

Or, worse, "provincial." I'm not sure that the poet has any control over that. I suppose even Robert Frost could have ended up being a regional poet, and that's how he was marketed at first. Luckily I have quite a few regions to call on and that's reflected in the way you have arranged this selection. Yes, I'm a poet of place. I tend to respond to wherever I am; but my imagination instinctively returns to Hounslow.

You grew up on the Heath. How did that region influence the poet you would become?

I always say that if you weren't lucky enough to be brought up in the Lake District as Wordsworth was, you have to make do with what you have. Seamus Heaney saw a poet's childhood as his or her capital. In my case "the Heath" is what I draw on, yes, though that's not the Schubertian delight that it sounds. In fact, what was Hounslow Heath is now chiefly Heathrow airport, but fortunately the area has depths of mythology that I have been able to tap, not least in my collaboration with Penelope Shuttle. It's associated with highwaymen, famously, but important historically too, since armies tended to muster there. It's also where Chamberlain took off for Munich to meet Hitler. And apparently a "druid" temple was discovered when they were laying the first runway—a story I make some use of in "Heath Row" (a poem, incidentally, which goes backwards) and in "Terminal".

For many years you've lived in a place that, in one sense, no longer exists—Huntingdonshire. What sort of symbolic influence does Huntingdonshire have over your imagination?

Yes, I suppose it is to me what imaginary Wessex was to Thomas Hardy. I rather like the idea that the shire I live in isn't there any more (it was merged with Cambridgeshire in the seventies), though you can't take a place away by renaming it. After all, I still hear my next-door neighbour talking with his distinct Huntingdonshire accent: his father actually used to walk behind a horse plough here. And Oliver Cromwell would have been surprised to learn that he was now a Cambridgeshire man. The county is historically important, especially with regard to the English Civil War, but it's rich in literary associations too—I've written about this in my book, *Vapour Trails*. George Herbert and John Donne both held the livings of local churches. William Cowper lodged in Huntingdon for some time. John Clare passed nearby on his famous walk home from the asylum in London. And T. S. Eliot's Little Gidding is a place I cycle to quite regularly.

Over the decades you've produced four stellar sequences based in or inspired by Huntingdonshire—the eclogues, the nocturnes, the elegies, and the codices. How did these sequences come about?

It began with the thirty-two "Huntingdonshire Eclogues" late in 1988. Unfashionably bucolic, they were nevertheless one of the most radical things I have written, and magazine editors really liked them. I was simply writing about "what happened" as Robert Lowell once advised. I suppose these poems were part of my determination to make something of my own back yard, having so often turned to the exotic, which is really rather easier. They were also a way of coming to terms with a landscape I was unsure about. I wanted to make myself really *look* and to use my own voice: so, I was, you might say, rediscovering the eye and the I. Curiously for such English poems, it was reading an essay by Seamus Heaney, "Englands of the Mind," that set me off.

Tell me more about the form of these poems.

The unusually long lines were learnt, I suspect, from reading that terrific American poet, C. K. Williams and encouraged by the arrival of my first ever word processor, which opened up all kinds of formal possibilities. The "Eclogues" were essentially in loose, unrhymed tercets, each one just fitting on a page. They were followed ten years later by "Huntingdonshire Nocturnes," more of a summer sequence, for the most part lit by moon and stars. This time there were forty-two poems in tercets, but of different lengths, more tautly composed with a six-beat line (still unrhymed). Another decade on, with the publication of *Hunts: Poems 1979–2009*, I wanted to bring the sequences together by adding a shorter group of new, rather autumnal "Huntingdonshire Elegies," now introducing some rhyme. That seemed to be that. But then in 2018 what looked like a trilogy became a "Huntingdonshire Quartet" with the arrival of 64 wintry "Codices," unashamedly literary, shorter, still in tercets and with that long six-beat line, but now very obviously rhyming. They haven't been published in full yet, but there are a few included here.

You also have some very different poetic interests, including a deep connection with German poetry.

I studied German (I can read it better than I speak it) and spent a year on a Studentship at Mannheim University. Because of my musical interests, it's been invaluable, and German literature has undoubtedly influenced me more than, say, French. It's only in the last ten years, though, that I've made serious attempts at translating Hölderlin, Rilke, and Goethe, so it's good that you have been able to represent them here.

I've also noticed an interest in Old Norse and Icelandic poetry—there's your *New English Edda*, for instance—and in Iceland more generally.

As for Iceland, that interest goes back to my father's spell as a wireless operator in Akureyri during World War II. He seldom talked about those years, but mentioned them enough for me to realise how important they had been to him. He had just got to know my mother when he was posted there, and she was living through the London Blitz. Nor did he ever return (I'm afraid he used to complain that it was "full of Americans") but a grant from the Society of Authors enabled me to make a pilgrimage there in 2001, soon after his death. I wanted to track down the RAF station where he was based, called—can you believe it?—Valhall Camp. The book that emerged, *Iceland Spar*, took its title from a piece of calcite I bought for our elder daughter, Katie, at the Natural History Museum in Washington. It's a stone which makes everything appear double, and as you have observed in your introduction, there's a lot of doubleness in my work. Anyway, I had a wider interest in Iceland, having studied Old Norse at Swansea where I wrote *Ragnarok*, that play about the gods.

And then there's "Coming Soon," which seems to be a remastering of Old Norse.

Ragnarok again. "Coming Soon" is an abridged adaptation of *Völuspá* ("The Song of the Sibyl"), the most apocalyptic of the *Poetic Edda*. Yes, I remastered or reimagined its vision of the end of the world in terms of a Hollywood disaster movie. Having written it during the summer of 2001, it was weirdly unsettling to be printing off the final drafts as the news came in of 9/11. It's a poem best read in one go, without worrying too much about what the names mean. I recommend Keats's "negative capability," with a touch of Coleridge's "willing suspension of disbelief." Inevitably, there are quite a few Icelandic words and mythological references, but the lists of gods and heroes can be treated as disposable extras in the overall epic. I have simplified and anglicised, much as Auden and Taylor did in their *Norse Poems*, pulling out the troublesome thorns.

Another "remastering," if you'll permit the term, is the Akhenaten poem, "To the Sun." Who was Akhenaten, and how did you come to write this poem?

Well, he's best known today as the subject of Philip Glass's minimalist opera. But to the Priests of Thebes (modern-day Luxor) he was the heretic pharaoh who decided that monotheism was the way forward, that everyone should be worshipping the solar disc, the "Aten." In fact, we know very little about him, despite the number of books (the same is true of Cleopatra, whose story I have recently been retelling) except that the Priesthood tried to erase him from history. But in the remains of his palace at Amarna, which we never visited, alas, among the extraordinary informal images of pharaonic family life, there's a *Hymn to the Sun*. Glass uses it in his opera, and it has long been attributed to Akhenaten himself. It's reminiscent of the Psalms—particularly Psalm 104—and hard to "translate" into anything other than a Biblical register. Over the years I had occasionally tinkered with the *Hymn* and tried to transmute it into something readably modern, less monophonic. *To the Sun* is very much a Lowell-style "imitation" in which I used elements of other translators' versions (I do not read hieroglyphics) to create a solar poem, whose source is Akhenaten, but which casts a few contemporary shadows.

I'm glad we've returned to considering Egypt. I have a few more questions about this. The whole world was interested in King Tut in the 1970s, but you seem to have made a particularly strong connection.

Another kind of mask, I suppose. I somehow identified with Tut, and felt a sequence of poems would work better than a play. But it all goes back to the Tutankhamun exhibition which came to London fifty years after the tomb's discovery. In 1972 I was eighteen, the same age as the pharaoh when he died, and the memory of queuing up to view the exhibits is what prompted my snaking sestina, "The Treasures of Tutankhamun," where UCCA is not an Egyptian god, but the Universities Central Council on Admissions—because I'm also waiting to know what my future holds.

That exhibit eventually made its way to the United States in 1977, and I clearly remember all the buzz of excitement though I was but a teenager. But you go further, and recreate the discovery of the tomb in the 1920s.

The story of how the tomb was discovered is well known. Lord Carnarvon (of Highclere Castle aka Downton Abbey) had for several seasons funded Howard Carter, son of a gamekeeper's son, in a series of excavations in the Valley of the Kings. It was very much at the last moment that the opening was found, and the event became a media sensation. Carnarvon died of a mosquito bite before the final coffin was opened. There are all kinds of resonances in the story for me. By coincidence, the *Champollion* which took Carter to Egypt was the very ship which took my father to Iceland during the Second World War.

Was your father equally afflicted with this new rage for Tutankhamun's treasures?

Oh yes, I remember him buying the Penguin best-seller about Carter's work, and encouraging me to attend that anniversary exhibition with my visiting German penfriend. One of the enduring treasures of our time in Upper Egypt was when my parents came to stay and we were able to take them to see all our own "wonderful things." Dad was a "brittle" diabetic, and when he suddenly fell ill for lack of sugar (though surrounded by sugar cane!) as we were all cycling to the Valley of the Kings, he was miraculously rescued by a stranger from the notorious tomb-robbing village of El-Gurnah. I describe all that in "For my Father." But there was so much to say about the Tutankhamun story: the class differences between Carter and Carnarvon, the various legends about a curse, and personal things like a memory of a little Tutankhamun after-dinner trick I had when I was a kid. I barely touched on the topic in my first book, *Westerners*, which was entirely about Egypt. That's why I ended up writing a separate Tut sequence. It was also a musical experiment—in variation form.

Music is extraordinarily important to you, isn't it, if you'll permit another diversion. Choosing a mere twenty or so poems demonstrating the hold music has on your imagination was a real challenge. To what extent do analogies between music and poetry hold true?

Dryden's definition of poetry as "articulate music" is one of my favourites. But you don't have to be musical to be a poet, as W.B. Yeats shows. He was tone deaf— and a surprising number of poets have been (Donald Davie comes to mind). I think one of the reasons I write poetry is because I can't compose, and there are all kinds of parallels between what a composer does and how a poem is created. Writing a long poem is the nearest I'll ever get to composing a symphony.

I like that analogy. I've extracted portions of your recent masterpiece, *The Silence*, here. Were you consciously thinking of yourself as composing symphonic music when writing your great long poem about Sibelius?

That was one of the delights of writing that poem. I ended up using rather Sibel- ian methods to compose it, cutting the whole thing savagely by almost half in a single afternoon. But there's a danger in becoming too overtly musical in poetry: you can turn into Swinburne or Dylan Thomas. Nevertheless, I'm a sucker for the musical delights of poets I don't fully understand—Wallace Stevens, for example, or Louise Glück. I'm sure it was the music of Eliot that won me over, and even now I have very little idea what's going on in some of the passages of *The Waste Land* that I have by heart.

Another long, almost symphonic poem, and one that many American readers may find curious, is *Fotheringhay*. How did this poem come about?

It came on a walk, as have several of my longer poems. I may even still have the ordnance survey maps covered with my scribbled drafts. I'm not the first poet to find that walking is conducive to writing—though Wordsworth, surprisingly, found his greatest inspiration on a long straight gravel path. I corresponded for a while with that fine American landscape poet Peter Kane Dufault, and he remarked of my poems—those he had seen—that they almost all involved a walk. Anyway, it was a glorious September day in 1989, and my sister-in-law was visit- ing from abroad with her new baby. I thought I'd escape the domestic scene for a while and drive half an hour into Northamptonshire. If you don't know England, one of the joys is the network of public footpaths, whereby you can plan a circular walk from anywhere to anywhere and you're always within your rights—even if the path crosses someone's back garden. This route had all the elements needed to spark a poem, especially Fotheringhay Castle, a scenic mound above the River Nene which marks the place where Richard III was born, but also where Mary, Queen of Scots was executed. There's a single lump of masonry there, and occasionally you'll find sprigs of heather or other tributes. There's hardly ever anybody about, but it's one of the most atmospheric places I know.

You are clearly interested in historic figures with outsized personalities. Omm Sety is one such figure. Who was she, and how did you go about telling her story?

Omm Sety was an English woman, Dorothy Eady, who became convinced, after a bad fall at the age of three, that she was in reality an Ancient Egyptian priestess from the Temple of Abydos. She even believed she had been the mistress of Sety I, and she spent much of her adult life living near the temple where she was something of an Ancient Marineress. It was a name we had heard friends mentioning when we were living in Aswan. One or two had even met her (she died the year we left). I wrote my poem about her much later, in the 1990s, drawn to the occult aspects of the story and to the various personal associations, but I wanted it to be formally quite different from *Westerners* or *The Tutankhamun Variations*.

The *Omm Sety* sequence reminds me of the importance of form in your poetry. This poem contains some of your more unusual and inventive stanza shapes.

Omm Sety is pretty bizarre in its construction—based on the layout of Abydos temple itself. The original pamphlet is over thirty pages, but we only include an extract here and life is too short for me to give much further explanation. Eliot got it right when he called poetry "a superior amusement." There's the satisfaction of setting yourself a puzzle and solving it, something I feel the Ancient Egyptians would have understood. Do you remember Archibald MacLeish's reply when Robert Frost asked him how he wrote? He said he bound himself in chains and then tried to get out of them. Frost remarked sourly that he couldn't have many readers.

In terms of form, you are one of the most extraordinarily versatile and dextrous of contemporary poets. You've written shaped poems, of course, but also villanelles, sestinas, and more sonnets than I can count. You write in long lines and short lines, in free verse, blank verse, accentual and syllabic verse. And you have an astounding facility with slant rhyme. Do you consider yourself a formalist? Do you have particular forms and meters to which you find yourself naturally drawn?

I'm certainly not a formalist, no, and I don't much like the term. I don't think, for instance, the American poets labelled formalists are necessarily the best at using form. The best are those who use it without the reader even noticing. A good poet must be ready to deploy everything, really, whatever seems right for the theme. Remember, Yeats used to write his poems out in prose first, and knew that you have to conceal all the hard work. "A line will take us hours maybe; / Yet if it does not seem a moment's thought, / Our stitching and unstitching has been naught." But, yes, the form is often what prises out the poem you didn't know you wanted to write—and they're often the ones that matter. You start off thinking you'll write about a song thrush, and the form keeps nudging you in a certain direction; it turns out that it wanted to be a poem about your grandfather. Syllabics can be good in that respect: you never know what the line breaks are going to throw up. I'm a great believer in line breaks, which is why I have difficulties with the prose poem. I've written plenty of short prose within poem sequences, but I wouldn't call any of it prose poetry. Do I have favourites? I have default modes—short unrhymed tercets, for instance, and I spend my life trying not to write blank verse, which is what free verse always aspires to. Free verse is unquestionably the toughest form. Anything that claims to be free is usually difficult.

As a poet with deep roots in verse drama, do you find yourself drawn to the persona poem or dramatic monologue? After all, your first poem was spoken by a duffel bag!

Ha! Let's call it doggerel. I remember Ted Hughes liking what he called the "holdall" quality of my early verse, so there must be something about bags. Many of my early poems are dramatic monologues, it's true—there's one spoken by Akhenaten (not included here), another stronger one by Nefertiti from *Westerners* which you did select. They're both in very short lines.

I have sometimes wondered if you had ever considered writing the Sibelius poem in the first person.

There are passages of it in the first person, where his voice merges with mine, and there's some direct speech. But I don't do monologues so much these days, although I've recently returned to them for my new *Cleopatra-Antony* sequence. Part of the process of writing all those Huntingdonshire poems was to restore confidence in the discredited narrative "I" after all the impersonality of Modernism. Really, it's hard not to sound like one of the Victorians or Robert Frost if you write dramatic monologues, though poets as diverse as Anthony Thwaite and Richard Howard have tried. Carol Ann Duffy (herself a dramatist) has led the field in the UK, and Dana Gioia has done it effectively in the US. But, as I've already suggested, it's best to cover your ears against the siren-call of the iambic pentameter. Having said that, there are a few blank verse speeches in this collection, usually for a good reason. "Richard III," for example, is a deliberate nod to Shakespeare, and was part of a Plantagenets sequence, chiefly monologues, which used a variety of forms.

How would you like your ideal reader to approach your work?

With an open mind, and an ear for the resonances of meaning, and the word music. The music and the imagery, the way they play against the form—that's crucial. It's a mistake, really, to think too much of what a poem is "about," and very often mine are not about what it seems they are. Those double meanings again. I would hope also that my readers might be pleasantly surprised, entertained, occasionally enlightened and even baffled, but enjoyably so. John Ashbery used to start his readings by saying "This won't hurt." But Pope nailed it when he wrote of "what oft was thought, but ne'er so well expressed." That's what I want readers to feel.

You once said to me that poets are really not always good judges of their own work. Do you still think that?

I do, and it's one of the reasons that I'm happy to let you edit me. It's quite unusual (unless the poet concerned is dead) but there's a lot to be said for it. I got to know Lowell, for instance, through Jonathan Raban's judicious selection for Faber aimed largely at a British readership. For one thing, poets tend to prefer their most recent work, and are inclined to omit anything faintly uncomfortable, or else do the opposite to prove that they are still at the cutting edge. Robert Graves was so determined not to be pigeon-holed that he declined to reprint much of his excellent war poetry. I've just edited the *Selected Poems* of the Hebridean poet, Iain Crichton Smith—he died in 1998 and is perhaps not very well known in the US—and found a huge number of good poems he had sidelined. There are a few anthologies where poets were invited to select their favourites—*Poet's Choice*, for instance, and *Let the Poet Choose*—and they are never what you'd expect. Edmund Blunden almost threw away what became one of his most celebrated poems, "Report on Experience."

Looking ahead, are there projects you are planning? Are there particular things you still hope to accomplish as a poet?

What do I hope to accomplish? Well, I have been known to quote Howard Nemerov's remark about "getting something right in the language." And it's true, that's what really matters to me—as you know, Kevin, from our late night WhatsApp exchanges about the placing of a dash or a line break. But then an idea will take hold of me. Last year, I found myself wanting to write something about Antony and Cleopatra, perhaps because of the "completist" in me: here was an obvious Egyptian theme I had barely touched, and one that centred on Alexandria, where so much began for me. On other occasions, as when I'm off on a writing retreat, I've consciously set myself a topic, or "sought a theme" like Yeats. That happened with the book-length sequences, *Knot* and *The Giddings*, both of which I composed at Hawthornden, where writers are expected to work in silence all day, so you'd go mad if you didn't have a plan. But I know that the best poems usually catch me unawares, often after a dry spell. Those sudden cloudbursts are like blessings, and they bring enormous satisfaction, especially if there's some formal game going on. "Aufklärung," the final poem you've included here, is one of those. To get me through the first Covid lockdown I had been listening to all 104 of Haydn's symphonies, and I suddenly needed to write a poem that replicated that playful, tuneful, life-affirming quality. I wrote 104 lines at one sitting, trying to deploy the particular word associated with the named symphonies at the relevant point (though I omit some of the less established titles). So, you'll find a surprise in line 94 and a farewell in line 45. Come to think of it, this book's opening poem, "Huntingdonshire Psalmody," also came out of the blue, during a walk from our house—one I do several times a month—on a perfect Spring day. It's a case of being ready to receive these gifts when they're offered, as I think Seamus Heaney once said. I recall that he also considered calling one of his later collections "Keeping Going." That's probably all any of us can do.

Thank you so much for this enlightening discussion. It's been a genuine pleasure.

April 27–30, 2021

Chronological Table of Contents

Poems from Collections

Uncollected Poems

Previously Unpublished Poems

Note

The following poems have been retitled or were originally untitled. Original titles, or the sequences from which the previously untitled poems have been extracted, are provided in parentheses.

Index of First Lines

Index of Titles

Biographical Notes

About the Author

John Greening was born in London in 1954 and studied at the universities of Swansea, Exeter and Mannheim (Germany). Apart from a spell working as a children's magician and then at BBC Radio 3, he has taught for much of his life. After two years with Voluntary Service Overseas in Aswan, Upper Egypt, and a period helping Vietnamese refugees in NE Scotland, he and his wife settled in Cambridgeshire where their two daughters were born, and where they have remained. In 1990–1991, they spent a year in New Jersey on a Fulbright Exchange. Since *Westerners* in 1982, there have been over twenty collections of poetry, including two from Carcanet, *To the War Poets* (2013) and *The Silence* (2019), as well as a series of recent pamphlets: *Achill Island Tagebuch* (2019), *Europa's Flight* (2019), *Moments Musicaux* (2020), *The Giddings* (2021), *a Post Card to* (with Stuart Henson, 2021) and *Omniscience* (2022). *The Interpretation of Owls* is John Greening's first American *Selected Poems*. Other books include studies of Yeats, Elizabethan love poets, Thomas Hardy, Edward Thomas and Ted Hughes, along with editions of the Hebridean poet, Iain Crichton Smith (*Deer on the High Hills*, 2021), and Geoffrey Grigson (*Selected Poems*, 2017). In 2015, he produced a major new edition of Edmund Blunden's classic memoir *Undertones of War* for Oxford University Press and he has written extensively about the First World War. In 2022 Arc published a selection of his translations from Goethe (*Nightwalker's Song*). There have been several anthologies, notably *Accompanied Voices: Poets on Composers from Thomas Tallis to Arvo Pärt* (Boydell, 2015) and *Hollow Palaces* (with Kevin Gardner, Liverpool University Press, 2021). In 2016 he collaborated with Penelope Shuttle on poems about the area near Heathrow airport, *Heath*, and the year after published a memoir, *Threading a Dream: A Poet on the Nile*. A series of personal meditations on his life in poetry (*A High Calling, or Where Do You Get Your Ideas From?*) is scheduled for publication by Broken Sleep in 2023. He has reviewed for the *Times Literary Supplement* since the 1990s, and his collected reviews and essays, *Vapour Trails*, appeared in 2020. John Greening's verse drama about the Lindbergh kidnap, *A Ladder in Hopewell*, was premiered in Asheville, North Carolina, in 2002. Musical collaborations include settings of his words by Cecilia McDowall and Philip Lancaster, contributions to Roderick Williams's Schubert Project (which was performed in Manhattan) and a libretto about Niagara Falls for the Dunedin Consort, premiered at London's Wigmore Hall. He was until recently Royal Literary Fund Writing Fellow at Newnham College, Cambridge. He has won the Bridport Prize, the Arvon Prize, the TLS Centenary Prize and in 2018 received a Cholmondeley Award from the UK Society of Authors for services to poetry.

About the Editor

Kevin Gardner is Professor of English and Chair of the Department of English at Baylor University in Waco, Texas. He received his BA from the University of St. Thomas in Houston, his MA from the College of William and Mary, and his PhD from Tulane University. He is a specialist in British literature of the eighteenth and twentieth centuries. He has edited several volumes of the poetry and prose of John Betjeman and an anthology of church elegies, *Building Jerusalem*. With John Greening, he has co-edited a collection of modern country house poems, *Hollow Palaces*, and the forthcoming *Contraflow*, a selection of poems from the last hundred years about Englishness.

A Note on the Front Cover Image and Frontispiece

This untitled picture was drawn and painted by the poet's grandfather, Clarence Melville Greening, in 1901. It is the inspiration for the book's titular poem, which can be read on pp. 173–74.